COMPREHENSION EXERCISES IN SOCIOLOGY

A D Burgen BA MLitt

Lecturer at Chester College of Further Education

Stanley Thornes (Publishers) Ltd

First published in 1982 by Stanley Thornes (Publishers) Ltd,
Educa House, Old Station Drive, Leckhampton Road,
CHELTENHAM, GL53 0DN

British Library Cataloguing in Publication Data

Burgen, Andrew D
    Comprehension exercises in sociology
    1   Sociology
    I   Title
    301   HM66

ISBN 0 85950 327 5

Phototypeset by Tradespools Ltd, Frome, Somerset
Printed and bound in Great Britain at Ebenezer Baylis, London and Worcester

CONTENTS

PREFACE

In public examinations in Sociology there is now an increasing emphasis on interpretative *skills* as opposed to mere reproduction of *received knowledge*. Examples of examinations using this approach include the Cambridge Local O-level, the new AEB O-level and the JMB A-level syllabuses. Question format typically consists of 'stimulus material' (statistical tables, textual extracts, even photographs) with a number of questions focusing on the interpretation of the presented material plus additional questions requiring sociological knowledge beyond that presented. The aim of this approach is to counter the rote learning of prepared answers. The hope is to allow candidates to show *both* their interpretative skills and their stock of sociological knowledge.

Examinations apart, there are also good pedagogical reasons for encouraging sound sociological analysis and comprehension. Teaching sociology is, after all, about teaching *insight* into social relationships and structure and not merely cataloguing and committing to memory statistics and sociological studies.

Thus, this book aims to give students practice in these skills, using a variety of stimuli and approaches. There is a wide variation in the *format* and *sophistication* of the exercises in this book. Many exercises go beyond mere 'testing' of students and seek to inform and generate insight as well. It follows that this book is *not* attempting simply to replicate the format of current or forthcoming examination questions. Teachers will quite naturally use past papers for specific examination practice.

To the sociology teacher this book should be of use in a number of ways:

(i) As stimulus or focal material The exercises could be used to introduce facets of sociological study (i.e. as discussion or seminar group topics which are then developed beyond the original exercise).

(ii) As a supplement to textbooks The exercises can be used as examples to illustrate general or theoretical points made in class (sources 'on tap'). Used in this way, the material would also be useful for A-level teaching as well as for O-level. It also introduces a 'skills' component to counterbalance the inevitable received learning.

(iii) As an evaluation of understanding In particular, the exercises can be used to enable the teacher (and the student) to determine how well the student has understood concepts or approaches. Can the student *apply* his or her knowledge to specific information or problems? This criterion applies even where candidates are sitting exams which consist purely of essay-type questions (i.e. no stimulus/comprehension questions).

A D Burgen
Chester 1982

ACKNOWLEDGEMENTS

The author and publishers are grateful to the following for permission to reproduce previously published material or for the provision of material:

Penguin Books Ltd, for extracts from *Invitation to Sociology* by Peter L Berger, *Racial Disadvantage in Britain* by David J Smith, 'Factory Time' by Dennis Johnson in *Work* edited by Ronald Fraser and *The Police* by Ben Whitaker

The Controller of Her Majesty's Stationery Office, for extracts from *Social Trends* 10 and 11

The Office of Population Censuses and Surveys for extracts from *Population Trends* 15, 16, 17 and 20 and *The Census Counts*

New Society, for the articles *Skinheads: The cult of trouble* by Ian Walker, *Social Trends: The rising popularity of cohabitation, Politics and Parties* by Michael Williams; and the diagrams used in report items 6.9.79, 2.4.81 and *Social Trends* 8.1.81 by cartographer Don Parry

Pan Books Ltd, for an extract from *Too Much Too Young* by Susie Fisher and Susan Holder

Laurence Pollinger Ltd and Penguin Books Ltd, for an extract from *Coming of Age in Samoa* by Margaret Mead

The Guardian, for the articles *Sterilisation Demand Overwhelms NHS* by Penny Chorlton, *Schools Swap Call by Williams* by Wendy Berliner and *Brixton's Morning After* by Mike Phillips

Times Newspapers Ltd and *The Sunday Times*, for the articles *Your Class Still Weights the Dice* by Elaine Potter, *Violent Britain: Myth or Reality?* by Phillip Knightley and Marjorie Wallace, and the illustrations and definitions which appeared in the feature *The 1:2:4 Rule of Class in Britain*

A M Heath & Co Ltd, for extracts from *36 Children* by Herbert Kohl and *Shooting An Elephant* by George Orwell (from *The Collected Essays, Journalism and Letters of George Orwell, Volume one*)

Longman Group Ltd, for extracts from *Race Relations in Britain* by Mercia Last and *British Government* by Philip Gabriel

Hutchinson Publishers Ltd, for an extract from *The Story of the Blues* by Paul Oliver

Encyclopaedia Britannica, for an extract from the article on 'Love' in the 4th edition

George Allen & Unwin (Publishers) Ltd, for an extract from *Fours Years Old in an Urban Community* by John and Elizabeth Newsom

National Foundation for Educational Research in England and Wales, for an extract from *A Survey of Rewards and Punishments (1952)*

Andre Deutsch, for an extract from *The Naked and the Dead* by Norman Mailer

Chatto and Windus Ltd, for an extract from *And Yet We Are Human* by Finn Carling

Fontana Paperbacks, for two extracts from *Racial Minorities* by Michael Banton

Oxford University Press, for an extract from *Race, Community and Conflict* by J Rex and R Moore

Holt, Rinehart and Winston, for an extract from *The Lugbara of Uganda* by John Middleton

Granada TV's World in Action programme, for the Ku Klux Klan material

Associated Newspapers Group Ltd, *The Guardian*, *The Daily Telegraph*, *The Sun*, *Financial Times*, London Express News and *The Times*, for their respective Brixton headlines

Syndication International, for the Brixton headline and the letter 'Not a joke' both from *Daily Mirror*

The United Nations Statistical Yearbook (1978) for the use of one of their tables

We also wish to thank the following who provided photographs:

Ian Berry and the John Hillelson Agency Ltd for the photograph on the title page of Inequality and Power

Fox Photos Ltd, for the photograph used on the title page of Deviance

Jennie Burgen, for the photographs on the title pages of the following chapters: Sociology; Family and Marriage; Education; Work and Leisure; Social Control; Race Relations; Beliefs (Two of these photographs are also used on the covers.)

Staff and students at Chester College of Further Education, for the photograph used on p. 96.

Picturepoint Ltd, for the photograph on the title page of Population.

Radio 210, for the use of its logo within the montage on the title page of Mass Media.

Every attempt has been made to contact copyright holders, but we apologise if any have been overlooked.

1 SOCIOLOGY

1A SOCIOLOGY AS A WAY OF LOOKING AT THINGS

In this extract Peter Berger gives an example of how sociologists try to look 'behind the scenes' of everyday occurrences that we take for granted.

In Western countries, and especially in America, it is assumed that men and women marry because they are in love. There is a broadly based popular mythology about the character of love as a violent, irresistible emotion that strikes where it will, a mystery that is the goal of most young people and often of the not-so-young as well. As soon as one investigates, however, which people actually marry each other, one finds that the lightning-shaft of Cupid seems to be guided rather strongly within very definite channels of class, income, education, racial and religious background. If one then investigates a little further into the behaviour that is engaged in prior to marriage under the rather misleading euphemism of 'courtship', one finds channels of interaction that are often rigid to the point of ritual. The suspicion begins to dawn on one that, most of the time, it is not so much the emotion of love that creates a certain kind of relationship, but that carefully predefined and often planned relationships eventually generate the desired emotion. In other words, when certain conditions are met or have been constructed, one allows oneself 'to fall in love'. The sociologist investigating our patterns of 'courtship' and marriage soon discovers a complex web of motives related in many ways to the entire institutional structure within which an individual lives his life – class, career, economic ambition, aspirations of power and prestige. The miracle of love now begins to look somewhat synthetic. Again, this need not mean in any given instance that the sociologist will declare the romantic interpretation to be an illusion. But, once more, he will look beyond the immediately given and publicly approved interpretations.

(From *Invitation to Sociology* by Peter L Berger, 1966)

1. 'As soon as one investigates, however, which people actually marry each other, one finds that the lightning-shaft of Cupid seems to be guided rather strongly within very definite channels of class, income, education, racial and religious background.' Explain this sentence, giving examples.

2. The author refers to 'ritual' in courtship. Give some examples of this.

3. 'It was love! We liked the same things, felt the same way. We were made for each other.' How might a sociologist like Berger interpret such a statement?

4. Berger talks about the sociologist looking '... beyond the immediately given and publicly approved interpretations.' Suppose a government minister declares that 'Poverty is a thing of the past in Britain.' How might a sociologist react to such a statement?

5. Why might some people feel threatened by sociologists?

census 1981 ✓

The census counts

Every ten years there is a national census to count the number of people. The Census Office asks every household to answer questions on a census form. The plans for the census are approved by Parliament.

The census counts . . .

- the number of people in each area

- the numbers of men and women and whether they are single, married, widowed or divorced

- how many children there are, how many teenagers, people in their twenties, thirties, forties . . . retired people and so on.

The census counts people by . . .

- the kind of housing they live in

- the country in which they were born

- the kind of job they do and how they travel to work.

WHY WE HAVE A CENSUS

The census is the only way to count everyone. Census results are used by a great many people and are available to everyone.

1. What are the uses of the census to the Government?

2. What are the uses of the census to the sociologist? How, if at all, do these uses differ from those of the Government?

3. As well as official statistics on population, sociologists also make use of Government statistics on other aspects of British society. Describe four of these.

4. Under what circumstances might a sociologist have to collect his or her own statistics rather than using official ones?

1C SOCIAL SURVEYS

The following extract describes why and how a market research firm set about finding out the attitudes and beliefs of teenagers on a wide range of issues.

Unlike market researchers, sociologists are not in the business of discovering markets for their clients' products. Nor do sociologists normally use the system of recruiting described in the extract ('random sampling' is normally used).

Nevertheless, many of the problems of conducting a sample survey are shared by both sociologists and market researchers.

The study was started in March 1980:

> You might be wondering who we are, and what our interest is in listening to teenagers. You might be wondering if we have a vested interest and who pays us to do it anyway? Well, we are not youth leaders, civil servants or members of the Salvation Army. We are market researchers, Susie Fisher and Susan Holder. We are conducting the study on behalf of a mixed bag of people – retailers, financial institutions and manufacturers – who believe, like us, that if you are going to design goods and services for kids then you ought to understand something more about their lives than whether or not they like Coca-Cola. Our research company specializes in work with kids so we were keen to do a basic study to see how they view their own lives. We wanted to understand their priorities, and we did not want to avoid issues such as money, shops, advertising and television, which tend to get left out of other surveys. The media love to sensationalize youth, the papers are full of horror stories about sex and illiteracy, vandalism and violence. We wanted to put these images behind us and go out and talk to the mainstream – the sons and daughters of all the people who go to work every day, shop at the supermarket and like to watch television in the evenings. People like us and people like you.
>
> We decided that kids change a lot during their teens, so it didn't make sense to try to cover every one or we'd have ended up with a superficial impression. We wanted the time to listen to the kids in detail, so we chose to talk only to teenagers who were at secondary school, that is from the age of eleven up to sixteen. This gave us a chance to see how

they change as they approach puberty and how they develop after-wards, but stopped short of following them into jobs and further education.

We were lucky, because the market research profession was already set up to recruit whoever we wanted to talk to. Behind every little office in London is a nationwide network of ladies of all ages and from all walks of life, who acted as agents to help us find exactly the kind of people we needed to interview.

If we had happened to need a group of women who take holidays in the South of France, dye their hair green and have birthdays in November, a good recruiter would have found them for us somehow! She might knock on doors, stand in the street, question her daughter's school friends or raid the WI. She would know the resources of her own neighbourhood better than we could.

For this survey, though, there were almost no restrictions. We wanted to talk to kids in general, across the country. We asked the recruiters to find us particular age groups and were careful to divide our sample equally between middle-class and working-class families. This was determined by a standard classification which depends on the occupation of the head of the household. Each recruiter was assigned either a group of boys or a group of girls and was asked to get as wide a range as possible, avoiding obvious biases such as recruiting them all from the local football team.

In the first part of the study we ended up with eight groups – 11–12-year-old girls from Windsor, 13–14-year-old girls from Culcheth in Lancashire, 14–15-year-old girls from Sheffield, 15–16-year-old girls from Roehampton. The boys were 11–12-year-olds from Manchester, 13–14-year-olds from Dagenham, 14–15-year-olds from Kilburn in London, and 15–16-year-olds from Leeds. Seventy-six per cent of the UK population lives in cities, and this survey is more a picture of urban than rural teenagers.

Putting kids together in groups their own age was a good way to get them to talk. Most of them were at different schools so they didn't know each other to begin with. They had to draw on common experiences to get into conversation. Some issues were difficult to talk about in a group, so we talked to another twelve teenagers in three-hour sessions on their own. These sessions were in Southampton, Eastcote, Newcastle upon Tyne and Bristol.

We didn't want the interviews to be biased because of our own personalities, so we asked three of our colleagues to help us, and in the end the interviewing team comprised three women and two men. Every session was tape recorded and transcribed so our analysis began with a pile of transcripts a foot and a half high!

People feel more at ease in surroundings not too different from those at home, but it would have been naïve to have expected teenagers to talk freely when Mum might have walked in at any moment. So interviewer and kids all met at the recruiter's house, shut the door firmly, and with plentiful supplies of food and canned drinks, and the floor littered with magazines, toiletries and chocolate bars, settled in for a four-hour session.

Each of the groups came back for another four-hour session a week later, and the feeling forged between the group members was so strong that no one failed to make it.

We started off with a rough checklist of the areas we wanted to cover, such as family, school, media, shopping, but this was only a base and the kids themselves chose what to talk about.

We established trust by talking ourselves, but we took care not to influence what the kids said any more than we could help. It is always possible to argue that while the kids we talked to were interesting, they might not be representative of teenagers in general. Obviously we couldn't interview every teenager in the UK, in order to put those we did see in context, but here again market research techniques came to our rescue. It is possible to select a sample who are statistically representative of the teenage population, and ask them to fill out questionnaires about their attitudes. This isn't as sensitive as talking to kids in person, but it can give you a lot of additional information.

For this purpose our network of recruiters dispensed 520 questionnaires from Torquay to Glasgow which the kids took away to their bedrooms and filled out in private. (The questionnaire included several cartoons with blank bubbles for the teenagers to fill in as they thought best. The samples throughout the book are some of the best ones that came in.) To give you an idea of the scale of the research – national opinion polls typically survey 1,000 people over an age range of 18–80 when they predict the election results. Our sample surveyed 520 people over an age range of six years. This means that any figures we quote are statistically representative of the teenage population and deviate no more than five per cent from the figure we would get if we interviewed every 11–16-year-old in the land.

In Britain, the working classes outnumber the middle classes by two to one, and our questionnaire sample followed the same ratio. It included children from one-parent families, only children, racial minorities and children with mothers who go out to work. The study was as complete as we could have made it.

(From *Too Much Too Young?* by Susie Fisher and Susan Holder, 1981)

1. Why would it be an 'obvious bias' if a 'recruiter' obtained all her assigned group '. . . from the local football team' (paragraph 5)?

2. What problems arise out of seeking opinions from individuals in a group setting?

3. 'We didn't want the interviews to be biased because of our own personalities . . .' (paragraph 8). Explain what this means.

4. 'Obviously we couldn't interview every teenager in the UK . . .' (paragraph 12). Why not?

5. Explain what the authors mean when they say that asking teenagers to fill out questionnaires '. . . isn't as sensitive as talking to kids in person, but it can give you a lot of additional information' (paragraph 12).

6. Why is it important that the social characteristics of the teenagers in the questionnaire sample were similar to those of the general teenage population?

ID   QUESTIONNAIRE DESIGN

The following are examples of various errors or faults in questionnaire design, wording and so on. Each example has at least one fault. All items are of the 'Please tick (√)' type.

Attempt to identify the fault(s) in the examples.

1. AGE

    under 18 ☐
    18–21 ☐
    21–30 ☐
    30–45 ☐
    45–65 ☐
    over 65 ☐

2. MARITAL/FAMILY STATUS

    Bachelor/Spinster ☐
    Widow/Widower ☐
    Divorced ☐
    Married With Children ☐
    Married Without Children ☐

3. What Class do you belong to?

    Upper Class ☐
    Middle Class ☐
    Lower Class ☐

4. How many cigarettes do you smoke a day?

    Less than 20 ☐
    20–40 ☐
    More than 40 ☐

5. 'Most people sense that equality for women is unnatural nonsense.'

    Strongly Agree   Agree   Disagree   Strongly Disagree
        ☐   ☐   ☐   ☐

6. 'K T Naydan would have made a great Prime Minister.'

    Agree ☐
    Not Sure ☐
    Disagree ☐

7. Would you like to live in Finland?

    Yes ☐
    No ☐

8. How frequently do you sleep with your spouse?

    Too Often ☐
    Average ☐
    Not Enough ☐

2 FAMILY AND MARRIAGE

2A   PARENTS AND CHILDREN

Margaret Mead's studies of societies in Samoa and New Guinea in the South Pacific are regarded as classics in social science writing. In this extract, she contrasts the relationship between children and adults in Samoa and America.

The close relationship between parent and child, which has such a decisive influence upon so many in our civilization that submission to the parent or defiance of the parent may become the dominating pattern of a lifetime, is not found in Samoa. Children reared in households where there are half a dozen adult women to care for them and dry their tears, and a half a dozen adult males, all of whom represent constituted authority, do not distinguish their parents as sharply as our children do. The image of the fostering, loving mother, or the admirable father, which may serve to determine affectional choices later in life, is a composite affair, composed of several aunts, cousins, older sisters, and grandmothers; of chief, father, uncles, brothers, and cousins. Instead of learning as its first lesson that here is a kind mother whose special and principal care is for its welfare, and a father whose authority is to be deferred to, the Samoan baby learns that its world is composed of a hierarchy of male and female adults, all of whom can be depended upon and must be deferred to.

Nothing could present a sharper contrast to the average American home, with its small number of children, the close, theoretically permanent tie between the parents, the drama of the entrance of each new child upon the scene and the deposition of the last baby. Here the growing girl learns to depend upon a few individuals, to expect rewards of life from certain kinds of personalities. With this first set towards preference in personal relations she grows up playing with boys as well as with girls, learning to know well brothers and cousins and schoolmates. She does not think of boys as a class but as individuals, nice ones like the brother of whom she is fond, or disagreeable, domineering ones, like a brother with whom she is always on bad terms. Preference in physical make-up, in temperament, in character, develops and forms the foundations for a very different adult attitude in which choice plays a vivid rôle. The Samoan girl never tastes the rewards of romantic love as we know it, nor does she suffer as an old maid who has appealed to no lover or found no lover appealing to her, or as the frustrated wife in a marriage which has not fulfilled her high demands.

(From *Coming of Age in Samoa* by Margaret Mead, 1928)

1. Explain the opening sentence, 'The close relationship ... Samoa'.

2. How does the Samoan child relate to his or her parents and to adults in general?

Explain the Samoan girl's attitudes towards sex roles and personalities (paragraph 2).

4. In about 200 words, discuss the importance of the family in Britain for the socialisation of the child.

2B   MEN AND WOMEN

The following extract comes from an article on 'Love' which appeared in the 4th edition of the *Encyclopaedia Britannica*, published between 1800 and 1810. This particular passage concentrates on the roles of men and women:

The man, more robust, is fitted for severe labour, and for field exercises; the woman, more delicate, is fitted for sedentary occupations, and particularly for nursing children. The man, bold and vigorous, is qualified for being a protector; the woman, delicate and timid, requires protection. Hence it is that a man never admires a woman for possessing bodily strength or personal courage; and women always despise men who are totally destitute of these qualities. The man, as a protector, is directed by nature to govern; the woman, conscious of inferiority, is disposed to obey. Their intellectual powers correspond to the destination of nature. Men have penetration and solid judgement to fit them for governing; women have sufficient understanding to make a decent figure under good government: a greater proportion would excite dangerous rivalship between the sexes, which nature has avoided by giving them different talents. Women have more imagination and sensibility than men, which make all their enjoyments more exquisite; at the same time that they are better qualified to communicate enjoyment. Add another capital difference of disposition: The gentle and insinuating manners of the female sex tend to soften the roughness of the other sex; and wherever women are indulged with any freedom, they polish sooner than men.

These are not the only particulars that distinguish the sexes. With respect to the ultimate end of love, it is the privilege of the male, as superior and protector, to make a choice: the female, preferred, has no privilege but barely to consent or to refuse. Whether this distinction be the immediate result of the originally different disposition of the sexes, or only the effect of associations inevitably formed, may be questioned; but among all nations it is the practice for men to court, and for women to be courted: and were the most beautiful woman on earth to invert this practice, she would forfeit the esteem, however by her external grace she might excite the desire, of the man whom she addressed. The great moral virtues which may be comprehended under the general term integrity are all absolutely necessary to make either men or women estimable; but to procure esteem to the female character, the modesty peculiar to their sex is a very essential circumstance. Nature hath provided them with it as a defence against the artful solicitations of the other sex before marriage, and also as a support of conjugal fidelity.

1. In your own words, summarise the roles of men and women as described in the passage.

2. As mentioned above, this passage was published in the early 1800s. How much has the role of women in Britain changed since then? Write an essay of about 400 words, including important political, legal, economic and social changes in your discussion.

2C   STERILISATION

Sterilisation demand overwhelms NHS

By Penny Chorlton

Sterilisation, of men and women, is the fastest growing trend in family planning but the Government is failing to meet demand, according to the latest research published yesterday.

Around one-third of all couples in their thirties or older are now opting for one partner to be sterilised. Although vasectomies are more common than sterilisations, the provision of the former is patchy and in some parts of the country can only be obtained privately.

These figures are based on a random survey of 900 women in the north and south of England and published in a book called Family Planning, Sterilisation and Abortion Services, published by the Policy Studies Institute.

Its author, Mrs Isobel Allen, said yesterday: 'There has been a move away from sterilisation being offered as a method of last resort.' Many couples were choosing an operation after having two or three children and completing their families.

She added that the 200 professional workers interviewed by researchers felt that the operations should be free and widely available. Instead, they either had to be paid for or obtained by joining long NHS waiting lists.

The research was funded by the Department of Health and aimed at discovering what had happened in the field of family planning since 1974 when birth control methods became freely available under the NHS.

More than half of those seeking abortions had used some method of contraception at the time they became pregnant. 'People don't become pregnant from lack of awareness,' she said, adding that those most at risk included the very young, the newly separated or divorced and the older women who thought they were menopausal or sub-fertile.

Of those seeking abortions, she said: 'They are not the irresponsible group of popular mythology. Indeed, most of them had grave doubts about it, saying that abortion was what other people do.' Doctors, appointments and the postal service often prolonged abortions unnecessarily, she said.

Copies available from PSI 1–2 Castle Street London SW1. Price £4.

(From *The Guardian*, 31 March 1981)

1. According to the article, which group is having the highest number of sterilisations: (*a*) men, (*b*) women?

2. What reasons can you think of for people choosing sterilisation rather than using birth control methods?

3. According to the article, which groups of people are most likely to be seeking abortions?

4. Explain the sentence in the last paragraph: 'They are not the irresponsible group of popular mythology.'

5. What are the principal factors affecting family size in contemporary Britain?

2D COHABITATION

Social trends

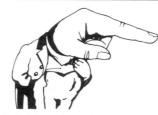

The rising popularity of cohabitation

Until very recently 'living together,' or cohabitation before marriage, was rare in nearly all European countries. The last major published survey in Britain (carried out in 1976) found that the proportion of couples who had cohabited before marriage was as low as 9 per cent. But the picture is now changing very rapidly in a number of European countries. 'Marriage without papers,' as Danish demographers have called it, is becoming the fashion.

So far, we know little about what's going on here. But some early figures from the 1979 General Household Survey, which included a new question about cohabitation, show that 20 per cent of women marrying in the late 1970s lived with their husbands before marriage. This compares with about 10 per cent of women married in the early 1970s. And at the time of the survey, 10 per cent of single women over 17 were living with someone 'as man and wife'.

These figures were released by the Office of Population Censuses and Surveys at a recent conference. We shall have to wait until later this year for a full analysis. But they fit intriguingly into what appears to be a European trend, though we are lagging behind Sweden and Denmark, and apparently well behind France.

In Sweden, pre-marital cohabitation appears to be almost universal, and there is a real possibility that large numbers of couples will not marry at all. About a third of all births are illegitimate, and a couple living together will not necessarily be precipitated into marriage by pregnancy. There's a similar trend in Denmark, though it is not so pronounced. Of those marrying in 1972, 80 per cent had previously lived together. A survey of 20–29 year olds (the age group which contains the majority of cohabitees) found that 25 per cent lived together in 1974. Married couples were much more likely to have children but a quarter of young people living together had children.

The French scene is rather different. There has been a rapid rise in pre-marital cohabitation. A 1977 sample survey shows an increase in the proportion of married couples who had lived together from 17 per cent of those wed in 1968–69, to 44 per cent of those wed in 1976–77. But the length of this cohabitation is quite short on average (just under 18 months) and it is almost invariably childless.

In France, there does not appear to have been a rejection of marriage altogether. Cohabitation is most popular with the 20 to 24 year olds, and the proportion of men and women married by the age of 30 (80 per cent of men and 84 per cent of women) did not change between 1968 and 1975.

There's a good deal of debate now about the significance of the cohabitation trend. Is marriage a dying institution which had its swansong in the 1960s, with an unprecedented popularity then? The rise in 'living together' can be seen as a symptom of the decline in the enthusiasm for, and social significance of, marriage. All over Europe, marriage rates (the proportions of young adults marrying by particular ages) have been falling, and average age at marriage has been rising. This trend began in Sweden and Denmark in the mid-1960s, spread to West Germany and Switzerland in the late 1960s, to Norway and England and Wales around 1970, and more recently to Italy and France.

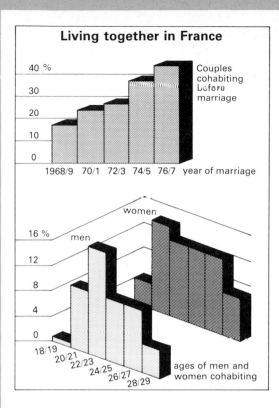

Living together in France

40 %
30
20
10
0

1968/9 70/1 72/3 74/5 76/7 year of marriage

Couples cohabiting before marriage

women

16 %   men
12
8
4
0

18/19
20/21
22/23
24/25
26/27
28/29

ages of men and women cohabiting

It could well be that there is simply a delay in marriage, related to economic factors. But there are other indications that the social significance of marriage has waned, as in Sweden and Denmark. For example, there appears to have been a general decline in shotgun weddings, as measured by the proportion of pre-marital conceptions legitimated by marriage. Illegitimacy carries less stigma.

However, outside Sweden, there is no very strong indication that the trend in living together is anything more than a step on the way to marriage. It corresponds to the phase of life in which previous generations moved from their parents' home to their marital home. It may well be that, as in France, a high proportion still marry by the age of 30, and that cohabitation is confined largely to the early and mid-twenties. We shall just have to wait to see what couples do in the 1980s.

In this context, the French 1977 survey of 18–29 year olds, carried out by the demographic institute, INED, is interesting. The target population covers the age group most likely to go in for what has been termed 'precocious cohabitation', to distinguish it from couples who live together when one (or both) is divorced or separated. (Cohabitation is common among the latter group in England and Wales.)

What kind of relationship?

As Louis Roussel, a commentator on the French findings, has pointed out, it is not easy to characterise this pre-marital living together. Should it be seen as a trial marriage, a form of engagement, a *union libre* (suggesting marriage has been rejected) or *concubinage* (which has a sleazy ring to it)? Just under a third of the couples in the French survey had lived together before marriage, and they were asked what sort of relationship they had had in mind when they first set up house. A third said they had planned to marry; a third that they hadn't made up their minds; a quarter don't seemed to have discussed the nature of the relationship; and only 7 per cent had been against marrige.

They all, of course, *had* married by the time of the survey. Those who had been undecided when they first lived together were asked what made them get married. About half said that by living together they'd found they could get on, so marriage was all right. About a quarter were expecting a child, and another quarter said that they had given in to social or familial pressures.

If, as many believe, the better-off are trend setters in social habits, then living together is going to become more fashionable. Among French cohabitees, there's a disproportionate number of the wealthier and better educated young adults, with Parisians leading the way. A very small-scale British survey in Reading in the early 1970s, when living together was rare, found that cohabitation was largely a social class I and II affair.

Whatever its social significance, living together appears to be spreading rapidly: a 1977 survey in Norway shows 30 per cent of 20–24 year old women cohabiting, and some Swiss figures for those married in Geneva in 1974–75 indicate that 60 per cent lived together before the wedding.

The European picture is far from complete, and fraught with difficulties of definition. How many live with one person, then marry another? What counts as cohabitation? And will younger cohabitees marry after a year or two? Before the 1960s, marriage signalled the start of sexual experience for the majority, and was a rough guide to the start of childbearing. This is no longer so. Will the link between living together and marriage disappear before the present decade is out?

(From *New Society*, 8 January 1981)

---

1. Is marriage a dying institution? Using the article as a basis for your discussion, write an essay of about 400 words.

Marriage and remarriage
Table 1

Divorce
Table 2

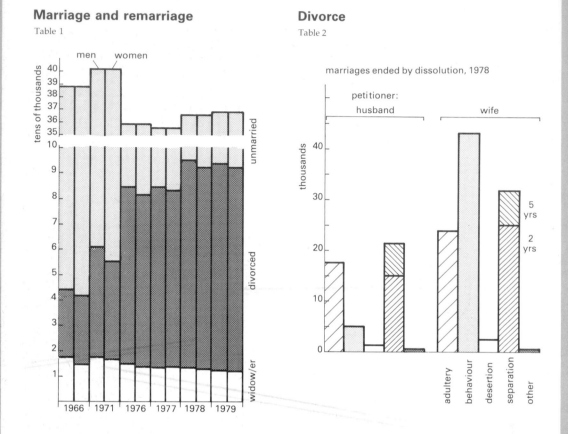

(From *New Society* 2 April 1981)   (From *New Society* 6 September 1979)

1. At first glance, Table 1 appears to show that there are fewer previously unmarried people getting married than divorced people remarrying in 1979. Examine the graph carefully and explain why this is *not* what it shows.

2. What change has there been between 1966 and 1979 in the number of divorcees remarrying? Why is there such a large change in the years after 1971?

3. According to Table 2, who is most likely to petition for divorce: (a) husband, (b) wife? What reasons can you give for this?

4. What is the most common reason for divorce for (a) wives and (b) husbands?

5. Explain why 'separation' is divided into '2 years' and '5 years'.

3 EDUCATION

Your class still weights the dice

If your father is in one of the professions or drawn from the high managerial classes, you stand an eleven times greater chance of getting a university degree than if he is a semi-skilled or unskilled worker. Nothing so very surprising about that except that a research study to be published next month by Oxford University Press will show that the effect of class on the sort of education a child gets is *increasing* rather than diminishing.

One of the main purposes of the study by Professor A. H. Halsey – part of a continuing project on social mobility at Nuffield College, Oxford – is to discover how far social and educational policies have succeeded in equalising 'life chances' in Britain. The title of his paper is in fact, 'Towards Meritocracy? The Case of Britain'.

Secondary education for all, free of financial handicaps, was enshrined in the 1944 Education Act in the expectation that through education there would be less waste of talent among working class children. Education, it was also thought, would play a crucial role in the formation of a more affluent and – perhaps – classless society.

To test the hypothesis, Professor Halsey considered the chances people had of going to a university, given their class origins, and he did this for those educated *before* and, *after* the 1944 act.

This entailed an analysis of the educational achievements and social origin of those men born between 1913 and 1931 and those born between 1932 and 1947.

Only 2.6 per cent of the total age group in the earlier years obtained university degrees while in the later years this rose to 6 per cent. Every social class group increased its output of graduates in the intervening years – but the proportions of graduates remained closely linked with social background. And the differences, surprisingly, were found to have increased rather than diminished.

Thus, while in the pre-Education Act years, 15 per cent of those boys in class one (professional and high managerial) obtained university degrees, 27 per cent of the post-Act generation obtained degrees. Similar increases were observed in class two. Groups seven and eight (semi-skilled/unskilled and agricultural workers) also increased their graduate prospects – from 0.9 per cent in each case to 2.4 and 1.8 per cent respectively.

But while the chances of graduation have risen more proportionately for the sons of unskilled and semi-skilled workers, the absolute percentage increases offer a more realistic picture. An extra 1.5 per cent of working-class children found their way to the universities after the 1944 Act compared with an extra 13 per cent of upper middle-class children.

What the table shows is that there is no clear trend towards the elimination of class inequality in educational attainment. The top class has fallen from having 5.76 times the average chance of getting a degree to 4.50 but the bottom class has worsened its previously disadvantaged position, from having just over to just under one-third of the average chance. Moreover, whereas before the 1944 Act above-average chances were shared by sons from the top four classes (amounting to nearly 30 per cent of the population) superior chances in the more recent period have accrued only to the sons of classes 1 and 2 (amounting to rather less than 15 per cent of the population).

No one knows precisely how open a society Britain was in the nineteenth century. There was, Halsey says, unquestionably some mobility between the generations, including leaps over the gulf which separated the manual class from the non-manual minority. But then capital accumulation, market acumen and on-the-job promotion accounted for a man changing his class – not education.

Now, however, qualifications matter and are doing so increasingly. A shift in occupational structure over the past generations has produced more opportunity at the top and more net upward mobility in our society as a whole. In other words, industrialised societies are gradually reducing their proportion of unskilled, low-paid jobs while increasing their sector of professional, technical and managerial occupations.

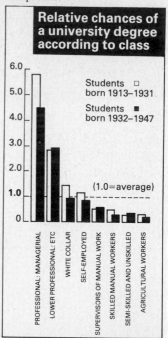

Relative chances of a university degree according to class

Students □ born 1913–1931
Students ■ born 1932–1947

(1.0 = average)

PROFESSIONAL: MANAGERIAL
LOWER PROFESSIONAL: ETC
WHITE COLLAR
SELF-EMPLOYED
SUPERVISORS OF MANUAL WORK
SKILLED MANUAL WORKERS
SEMI-SKILLED AND UNSKILLED
AGRICULTURAL WORKERS

The table shows that, with the earlier students, the professional classes had 5.76 times the average chance of getting a degree and that this fell later and that in the earlier group, the top four classes had a better than average chance of a degree but in the later group only the top two groups benefited in this way.

Encouragingly, the study shows that people are chosen for jobs less in terms of what their fathers did and more on what qualifications they themselves have managed to achieve.

At the same time, the family into which a child is born is actually having an increasing effect on the sort of education he receives. 'Class' says Professor Halsey, 'weights the dice of social opportunity and "the game" is increasingly played through strategies of child rearing which are umpired by schools. The direct effect of the class hierarchy of families on education opportunity has *risen* since the war.'

Another reason for the growing discrepancies between the classes, Halsey believes, is that schools are less immersing than they used to be. Thus the degree to which people are or are not educationally successful is less under the control of schools and school teachers than it used to be, and what happens within the family is commensurately more important.

The Halsey evidence is history. the analysis is about people who have already gone through the system and does not take account of the impact of comprehensive education.

But it seems to suggest that the simple expansion of educational opportunity is, on its own, not enough to make significant inroads into class biased educational disadvantages, a view shared by some American researchers. In an American study published in 1973, Raymond Boudon argued that evidence from a wide range of industrial countries was consistent with the theory that educational expansion and even the reduction of inequality of educational opportunity did not reduce the link between a son's social status and that of his father.

At the same time the growing importance of education as an influence independent of the family, enabling people to get jobs which reflect their educational attainments rather than their social origins, augurs well for the long term.

In the meantime, Halsey believes 'social and educational policy have not successfully seized on the enlarged occupational opportunities since 1945, in such a way as to realise either an egalitarian or a meritocratic society.'

Elaine Potter

(From *The Sunday Times*, 9 January 1977)

1. In your own words, describe one of the main purposes of Halsey's study.

2. What was expected to result from the 1944 Education Act?

3. How is the occupational structure changing in industrialised societies?

4. What does the study say about links between education and social mobility?

5. In about 50 words, summarise the study's main findings about the relative chances of getting a university degree for students from different social backgrounds.

6. List at least five factors in the student's home background which influence educational achievement.

Schools swap call by Williams

By Wendy Berliner,
Education Staff

Pupils at leading independent schools should study at a comprehensive and live-in with a family for at least a term, Mrs Shirley Williams said yesterday.

In return, comprehensive pupils should attend an independent school as boarders, she told the annual conference in Sheffield of the secondary heads association.

Such a scheme would prevent the social segregation caused by the two sectors of education, said Mrs Williams in her first speech on education since the formation of the Social Democratic Party.

Two schools could be twinned under this arrangement and the children swapped in the same way that continental exchanges take place. Eton, for instance, was 'a large comprehensive school' and it could twin with another large comprehensive.

Mrs Williams said: 'We accept exchanges between other countries and, sadly, Britain is two countries now. It sounds a bit wild but most things that are new sound wild in this country.'

Mrs Williams is the only member of the Gang of Four who wants fee-paying education abolished and it is unlikely that a Social Democratic government would abolish the independent schools.

She admitted yesterday that the nearest her colleagues were willing to come to her view was to support integration between the two sectors and an examination of charitable status which gives even the wealthiest schools perks such as cheap rates.

Mrs Williams said there were 'few more thorny problems than the relationship between state and independent schools'. She would be 'less than honest' if she did not say that some of the independent schools were excellent.

But the independent schools would also not be honest if they did not accept that there were bad ones among them, she added.

Britain was a highly socially-segregated society and segregation was passed from school to work to a far greater degree than its industrial competitors. The success of American schools owed a lot to the fact that the managing director's child would learn with the child of a factory worker.

Alienation between the two sectors was made worse by the assisted places scheme and the relative decline in resources for state schools.

Many independent school heads were concerned about the gulf between the two sectors. 'More and more people are getting fed up about the social segregation in Britain,' said Mrs Williams.

In a speech which sowed the first public seeds of SDP education policy, Mrs Williams said she believed that the maintained sector of education should provide a wider choice.

There should be room for boarding, denominational and both traditional and progressive education. For instance, parents should be able to choose a school that did not use corporal punishment.

The generation of schoolchildren from 'the bulge' years had been cheated at every turn, she said, with overcrowded classrooms, followed by rapid teacher turnover and now restricted opportunities because of the cuts.

'Unless we are very careful, we are going to be looking at a half-lost generation,' she said.

(From *The Guardian*, 31 March 1981)

1. Mrs Williams claims that her scheme would prevent 'the social segregation caused by the two sectors of education' (paragraph 3). Explain in about 50 words what you think she means by this phrase.

2. Eton, a public school, is referred to as 'a large comprehensive school' (paragraph 4). How much do you agree with this assessment?

3. What recent failings does Mrs Williams criticise the state ('maintained') sector of education for?

4. Write a sociological essay on Mrs Williams' scheme, discussing both the potential benefits and the potential drawbacks for pupils, for schools and for the country as a whole.

3C REJECTS

The following September meant meeting new children, concentrating my energy and feelings on them and letting go of my pre-occupation with the thirty-six children. It was sad yet exciting, beginning again with an empty classroom. I waited nervously for the children, refusing to think of my first words. At nine o'clock they came in quietly and hesitantly, looking me over. They were nervous too. I looked at my new class and told them how strange it felt to be in school again, starting another year, meeting new people. They agreed. One boy said he almost stayed at home. A girl, Alice, said she came because she knew that she'd be having a man teacher. At that I introduced myself and asked the class to sit in any seats they liked. Everyone looked at me, puzzled. Then a big boy, Willie, said:

'You mean I don't have to sit in the back?'

'No.'

'And you're not going to keep me at your desk to watch me?'

'Why, should I watch you?'

'Didn't they tell you?'

'Nobody told me anything about the class, I didn't ask. This is a new year, everyone starts from the beginning.'

Our first day of school was not like my first day with 6–1. I felt free to encounter the children without preconceptions and explore with them what was meaningful to learn. The children didn't frighten me; there was no question of control since I knew I was in control of myself. Time and chaos weren't my enemies—a bit of disorder, time to explore and play were all expected to be part of our year together. I had no trouble talking to the class. In a sense we started together and therefore could plunge into things more quickly than was possible with 6–1.

Other teachers had warned me of my new class—it was 6–7, 'the bottom'. I was told that the children were illiterate, indifferent, dangerous. Someone claimed that most of them wouldn't even show up after the first week. In June some colleagues, as the children suspected, offered to point out 'the ones' who would cause me the most trouble. I declined just as I had declined to look at the children's record cards in September.

The children looked older than the ones in 6–1, taller and more self-assured. They spoke about themselves freely and with great perception. They knew that they were rejects in the school, and they also knew that the school as a whole was a reject. Any adult pretence of the opposite would have closed them up altogether.

As soon as everyone was settled I began as directly as possible and asked the class what books they wanted to read. Naturally they asked for sixth-grade readers. I told them I felt the books were too hard and they groaned.

'We're not so dumb, Mr Kohl.'

'I won't do that baby stuff again.'

'Mr Kohl, we can read anything.'

I asked the children how well they thought they read and they became confused; no one had ever told them. They only knew that every year they got the same second- and third-grade books, which they knew by heart. My first lesson became clear. I took out the class record cards and dumped them on my desk. Then I explained to the class what grade-reading scores meant, and what the significance of IQ was.

'If you are reading your grade level, that means the sixth grade, you're supposed to have a score in the sixes; six point zero, six point one, and so forth. If you have average intelligence your IQ should be at least one hundred. Let's see what these cards say.'

There was suspense in the room as I listed the scores: 3.1, 3.4, 2.0, 4.2, 3.1 . . . IQ's of 70, 75, 81, 78 . . . then anger.

'Mr Kohl we're not that dumb.'

'It's phoney.'

'No one taught us that stuff, no one ever told us.'

But they knew now. After a heated debate I threw my first question back to the class.

The class chose fifth-grade books, ones they knew would be difficult for them in preference to ones that were on their supposed 'level'. They were ready to fight to read and learn, met my challenge, and kept on challenging themselves and me for the rest of the year.

One day during the first week Alice coyly proposed a bet.

'Mr Kohl, I bet I can read anything on your desk no matter what those cards of yours say.'

Her reading score was 3.4. I accepted and she went through all the books on my desk including a page of the novel I was reading on the way to school. I was perplexed and delighted.

'How can you do that and still have a three point four reading score?'

'I wouldn't read for those teachers. Listen—'

Alice picked up a book and stumbled through several paragraphs. She paused, stuttered, committed omissions and reversals, i.e., read on a low third-grade level. Then she looked at my astonished face and burst out laughing.

Alice was tough and angry and brilliant. She was hypersensitive and incapable of tolerating insult or prejudice. In her previous years in school she had been alternately defiant and withdrawn. She was considered a 'troublemaker' by some teachers, 'disturbed' by others. Yet when offered something substantial, a serious novel, for example, or the opportunity to write honestly, she blossomed. During the year she became hungry to learn and less hostile. It was sometimes hard to find material to keep up with her voracious appetite.

(From *36 Children* by Herbert Kohl, 1968)

1. Why are both the teacher and the pupils nervous when they first meet each other? Why is this nervousness interesting to the sociologist?

2. Both the children and the other teachers expected Mr Kohl to 'find out'

about his new class before he actually met them. What would have been the likely results if he had done so?

3. Do you think that teachers should tell pupils their IQs, reading scores, and so on? What are the advantages and disadvantages of doing this?

4. Why might Alice's case be interesting to a sociologist?

5. 'Intelligence is the main factor in educational success.' Discuss.

3D READING BETWEEN THE LINES

In the early 1970s, several studies were published on the portrayal of males and females in school reading textbooks (what the British call 'readers').

Studies of widely-read reading textbooks in the USA and Canada showed that the stories in them were 2½ times more likely to be centred on boys than on girls. There were 3 times as many stories containing an adult male character compared to stories containing an adult female character. Male biographies appeared 6 times more often than female biographies. The boys portrayed in stories were much more likely than the girls to be constructive, creative, inventive, strong, brave, competitive, independent and fearless.

A study of reading schemes in the UK found that these 'readers' were 'peopled with tea-drinking, domestic women and car-tinkering, breadwinning men'.

1. What effects might the themes in the reading textbooks mentioned above have upon the attitudes and beliefs of the children who read them?

2. A number of teachers objected to the way that sexual and racial differences have been portrayed in many school textbooks. Should sexes or races be portrayed as equals in school books? Or is this unnatural or unrealistic?

3. As a result of pressure from teachers and others, many textbooks with strong sexual or racial bias in them have been withdrawn. However, the American Jonathan Kozol claimed that the '. . . books are not issued any more – but the teachers still are . . .' What do you think he meant by this?

4. You sometimes hear people (often a 'TV personality') saying that 'the schools are to blame' for increasing juvenile crime and rebellion. How might schools be 'to blame'?

AFTER SCHOOL...?

Destination of school leavers: by sex

	England & Wales					As a percentage of all leavers				
	Boys					Girls				
	1966 /67	1970 /71	1975 /76	1977 /78	1978 /79	1966 /67	1970 /71	1975 /76	1977 /78	1978 /79
Pupils entering full-time further education as a percentage of all school leavers – by type of course:										
Degree	8·9	9·0	8·8	8·7	8·7	4·3	5·3	5·4	5·8	6·0
Teacher training	1·5	1·3	0·5	0·2	0·2	5·1	5·2	2·2	0·9	0·9
HND/HNC	0·7	0·7	0·4	0·4	0·4	0·2	0·3	0·3	0·3	0·3
OND/ONC	0·5	0·6	0·9	0·6	0·5	0·3	0·4	0·5	0·5	0·3
GCE 'A' level	1·2	1·6	1·8	1·9	1·9	1·0	1·1	2·1	2·2	2·3
GCE 'O' level	1·6	1·7	1·5	1·4	1·3	1·3	1·1	1·5	1·8	1·7
Catering	–	–	0·5	0·5	0·4	–	–	1·0	1·2	1·2
Nursing	–	–	–	–	–	–	–	1·6	1·4	1·5
Secretarial	–	–	–	–	–	–	–	4·8	5·3	4·9
Other full-time	3·6	4·7	4·5	4·0	3·7	8·9	10·8	6·0	6·4	6·8
Total pupils entering full-time education										
(percentages)	18·0	19·5	18·9	17·8	17·2	21·1	24·1	25·4	25·8	25·9
(thousands)	55·0	61·6	68·7	70·3	68·5	61·0	72·0	87·1	96·4	98·6
Total school leavers seeking employment on leaving school										
(percentages)	82·0	80·5	81·1	82·2	82·8	78·9	75·9	74·6	74·2	74·1
(thousands)	251·0	253·8	295·1	324·6	331·1	227·9	226·1	256·4	277·1	283·0
Total school leavers										
(=100%)	100	100	100	100	100	100	100	100	100	100
(thousands)	305·9	315·3	363·9	394·9	399·6	288·8	298·1	343·6	373·6	381·6

Source: Statistics of Education Vol 2, School Leavers CSE and GCE.
Department of Education and Science

(From *Social Trends* 11, 1981)

1. Compare the percentages of boys and girls taking degree courses between 1966/67 and 1978/79.

2. What is the approximate ratio of the percentage of girls to boys taking teacher training courses during this period?

3. As well as teaching, what other courses are taken by a much higher percentage of girl school leavers than boys? What do you think are some of the reasons for this?

4. Were the same *number* of girl school leavers taking OND/ONC courses both in 1966/67 and 1978/79?

5. Write an essay of about 300 words, describing what factors may lead school leavers either to choose the various courses listed in the table or to leave full-time education and seek employment.

4 INEQUALITY AND POWER

4A LIFE CHANCES

Sociologists are interested in the way that social structure affects the behaviour and opportunities ('life chances') of individuals and groups. 'Life chances' include the opportunities to achieve power, prestige, privilege and possessions. Life chances also literally mean one's chances of life and death. In Britain, people from different social backgrounds have different chances of surviving infancy, of suffering disease and disablement, and of surviving to a ripe old age.

The following table looks at the varying chances of survival of infants from different social classes:

Stillbirth and Infant Mortality rates in the first year of life for legitimate births 1975–77 by social class

Rate	Social Class						
	All	I	II	III (non-manual)	III (manual)	IV	V
Stillbirth (per 1000 live and still births)	9·5	7·0	7·7	8·6	10·1	11·1	13.4
Infant Mortality (per 1000 live births)	13·6	9·8	10·9	11·5	13·3	15·9	21·9

1. What is meant by 'stillbirth'?

2. In which social class is there the highest rate of still births?

3. Describe the pattern of infant mortality by social class.

4. What explanations can you offer for these class differences in stillbirth and infant mortality rates?

5. A National Health Service aiming to provide health care for all has been in existence for over 30 years. Do these continuing class differences in infant mortality mean that the NHS has failed?

Distribution of gross weekly earnings[1], April 1979

Great Britain

Percentage with gross weekly earnings in £1 earnings groups

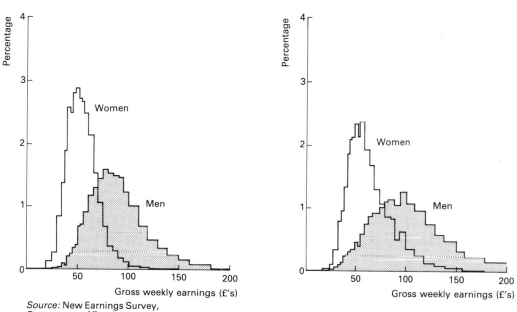

Manual employees

Non-manual employees

Source: New Earnings Survey,
Department of Employment

[1] Of full-time employees aged 18 and over whose pay for the
survey period was not affected by absence.

(From *Social Trends* 11, 1981)

I. Using the information in the charts, describe the main differences between the earnings of men and women and between manual and non-manual employees

2. In 300–400 words, explain why these differences exist.

Distribution of income[1] before and after tax, 1949 to 1977–78

United Kingdom
Income shares of selected quantile groups
Quantile groups

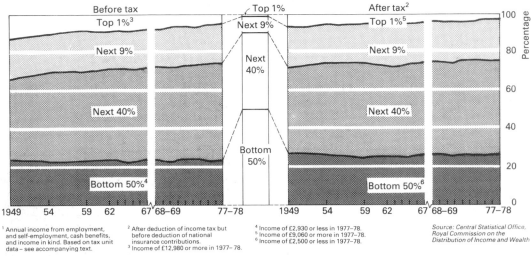

¹ Annual income from employment, and self-employment, cash benefits, and income in kind. Based on tax unit data – see accompanying text.

² After deduction of income tax but before deduction of national insurance contributions.

³ Income of £12,980 or more in 1977–78.

⁴ Income of £2,930 or less in 1977–78.
⁵ Income of £9,060 or more in 1977–78.
⁶ Income of £2,500 or less in 1977–78.

Source: Central Statistical Office, Royal Commission on the Distribution of Income and Wealth

(From *Social Trends* 11, 1981)

1. What is the difference between income and wealth?

2. If everyone received the same income, the lines on all three columns on the chart would line up. However, this is not the case. What percentage share of incomes before tax did the Bottom 50% have in 1977/78?

3. What percentage share of incomes before tax did the Top 10% have in 1977/78?

4. What changes in the distribution of incomes before tax have occurred between 1949 and 1977/78?

5. Many people believe that the taxation system, in which the rich have to pay higher rates of tax than the low-paid, helps to redistribute income ('robbing the rich to pay the poor'). Compare the income shares before tax and after tax. What differences has taxation made?

6. Footnote 1 refers to 'cash benefits' and 'incomes in kind'. Give examples of both of these.

4D   SOCIAL MOBILITY

The Oxford Social Mobility study has already been referred to in Exercise 1 of the chapter on Education. This brief newspaper extract is concerned with the origins and destinations of people on the 'social ladder'.

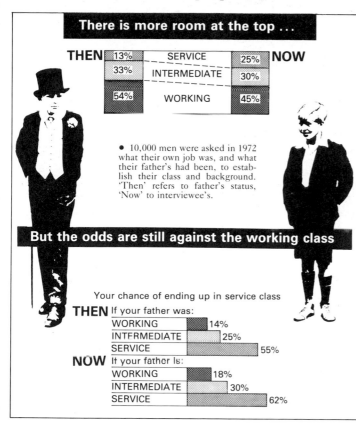

- More children from working class families reach the top now—but even more top children stay there. 'Then' refers to interviewees born 1908–17. 'Now' to those born 1938–47.

- 10,000 men were asked in 1972 what their own job was, and what their father's had been, to establish their class and background. 'Then' refers to father's status, 'Now' to interviewee's.

- The classes in the Oxford Social Mobility are divided into:

Service class: people with well-paid jobs with career prospects in the professions, national and local government, senior management and higher technical jobs.

Intermediate class: people with routine non-manual (mainly clerical) jobs; sales personnel; self-employed 'petty bourgeoisie'; supervisors; lower-grade technicians.

Working class: skilled and unskilled manual workers, including farm labourers.

(From *The Sunday Times*, 13 January 1980)

1. Give one example of a specific job (other than those mentioned) from each of the three classes used in this study.

2. How much has the 'service class' increased over the time covered by the study?

3. What chance would a manual worker's son born 1938–47 have of reaching the 'service class'?

4. What reasons can you give to explain why the sons of fathers in the service class stand the best chance of ending up in the service class themselves?

In the present parliament, 67 per cent of Conservative MPs went to public school compared with 3 per cent of the population as a whole. Nearly 15 per cent had been to Britain's top public school, Eton. A total of 48 per cent of Conservative MPs went to Oxford or Cambridge, whereas only 5 per cent of the population have been to any university.

In contrast, nearly 90 per cent of Labour MPs attended state schools and only 20 per cent went to Oxford or Cambridge. Thirty-two per cent of Labour MPs went to non-Oxbridge universities, compared with 17 per cent of Tory MPs.

Occupations of MPs

	Con	Lab	Lib	other
barristers	54	21	—	1
solicitors	16	10	—	1
journalists	31	19	1	1
publishers	5	—	—	—
public relations	2	—	—	—
teachers	14	53	3	4
medical	3	5	—	—
farmers, landowners	25	2	2	1
company directors	82	1	2	—
accountants	12	4	1	—
brokers	17	—	—	—
managers	52	33	—	2
architects	5	1	1	—
scientists	1	5	—	—
economists	8	9	—	1
banking	12	—	—	—
diplomatic	2	1	—	—
social workers	1	3	—	—
civil servants	—	3	—	—
local government	1	2	—	—
clerical and technical	1	3	—	—
engineers	8	30	1	—
mineworkers	—	16	—	—
rail workers	—	9	—	—
other manual workers	—	7	—	2
trade union officials	1	27	—	—
party officials	12	5	—	—
hoteliers	—	—	—	2
other jobs	10	5	—	—
ministers of religion	—	—	—	2

(From *New Society*, 13 March 1980)

1. What percentage of the following had been to any university: (a) Conservative MPs, (b) Labour MPs, (c) the general population?

2. List the top five occupations of: (a) Conservative MPs, (b) Labour MPs.

3. The Labour Party claims to represent the working class in Britain. How much does the educational and occupational background of Labour MPs reflect this working-class representation?

4. As well as social classes, what other social groups are under- or over-represented in Parliament?

5. What are some of the principal ways in which an individual can have an influence on the government of Britain?

4F PRESSURE GROUPS

Save the Avon Gorge

In 1971 Bristol Corporation gave permission for a company to build a large hotel in the Avon Gorge, a steep-sided valley of outstanding natural beauty. The hotel was to be situated close to the famous and spectacular Clifton Suspension Bridge, built by Isambard K. Brunel in the nineteenth century.

The planning permission was discovered by a member of a local society concerned with perserving the character of the area. Without delay a meeting was called to discuss opposition to the scheme. It was attended by about twenty people, who called themselves STAG (Save the Avon Gorge). Local MPs were contacted, and questions asked in the Commons. The Minister for the Environment and the press were invited to investigate the matter, and posters and car stickers were distributed. Before long, letters of support were pouring in, and a petition was started. Various public figures were asked to help, and among others John Betjeman, the poet laureate, came to Bristol.

The Minister set up a public enquiry, conducted by a planning inspector. It opened in May 1971 and lasted nine days. Opposing the hotel scheme were the National Trust and various local councils, together with individual architects and engineers. On the other side were Bristol Corporation officials, hotel representatives and some architects. In October the Minister accepted the findings of the Enquiry and permission to build the hotel was refused. STAG had won.

This case illustrates an important point about 'one issue' pressure groups. STAG won not so much because of the volume of public protest but because it managed to attract influential supporters. Most of its members were middle class, professional people, who knew how to organise themselves effectively and where to exert pressure.

(From *British Government* by Philip Gabriel, 1974)

1. In what ways was pressure put on Parliament by STAG?

2. In what other ways did STAG promote its cause?

3. It wasn't so much the *number* of supporters that STAG had, it was the *kind* of supporter. Explain in your own words how this was so.

4. What is a 'one-issue' pressure group?

5. Apart from the 'one-issue' pressure group, what other main type of pressure group is there? Give examples.

6. 'Pressure groups are the means whereby anyone in Britain can have their say and influence decisions made about life in Britain.' Discuss.

5 WORK AND LEISURE

Employees In employment: by industry

United Kingdom

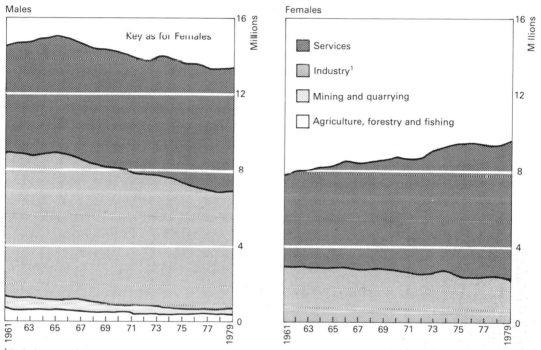

Males

Females

Key as for Females

Services

Industry[1]

Mining and quarrying

Agriculture, forestry and fishing

[1] Includes manufacturing: gas, electricity, and water; and construction industries: and for females also includes agriculture, forestry and fishing; and mining and quarrying.

Source: Department of Employment

(From *Social Trends* 11, 1981)

1. What changes have taken place in the total numbers of working men and working women between 1961 and 1979?

2. In which economic sector was there the highest number of females in 1979? Give examples of the kinds of jobs involved.

3. Why are there so many females in the sector referred to in Question 2?

4. In about 400 words, describe *and account for* the changes that have taken place between 1961 and 1979 in the number of men and women working in different economic sectors.

Factory Time

I work in a factory. For eight hours a day, five days a week, I'm the exception to the rule that life can't exist in a vacuum. Work to me is a void, and I begrudge every precious minute of my time that it takes. When writing about work I become bitter, bloody-minded and self-pitying, and I find difficulty in being objective. I can't tell you much about my job because I think it would be misleading to try to make something out of nothing; but as I write I am acutely aware of the effect that my working environment has upon my attitude towards work and leisure and life in general.

My working-day starts with that time-honoured ritual known as 'clocking-in'. In a job such as mine this is one of the more constructive acts of the day. For the uninitiated: a lever is pressed and, in blue ink, a time is recorded on one's card. It's so mechanical that one expects the time to be always the same. But it isn't. Just have the effrontery to be late: then you will find that your time has been stamped in RED ink. The management may condone bad timekeeping, but that blasted clock seems to shed blood in anguish.

After clocking-in one starts work. Starts work, that is, if the lavatories are full. In an hourly paid job it pays to attend to the calls of nature in the firm's time. After the visit to the lavatory there is the tea-break to look forward to; after the tea-break the dinner-break; after the dinner-break the 'knocking-off' time. Work is done between the breaks, but it is done from habit and is given hardly a passing thought. Nothing is gained from the work itself – it has nothing to offer. The criterion is not to do a job well, but to get it over with quickly. Trouble is, one never does get it over with. Either one job is followed by another which is equally boring, or the same job goes on and on for ever; particles of production that stretch into an age of inconsequence. There is never a sense of fulfilment.

Time, rather than content, is the measure of factory life. Time is what the factory worker sells: not labour, not skill, but time, dreary time. Desolate factory time that passes so slowly compared with the fleeting seconds of the weekend. Monday morning starts with a sigh, and the rest of the working-week is spent longing for Friday night. Everybody seems to be wishing his life away. And away it goes – sold to the man in the bowler hat.

People who speak grandiosely of the 'meaning of work' should spend a year or two in a factory. The modern worker neither gives anything to work nor expects anything (apart from his wages) from it. Work, at factory level, has no inherent value. The worker's one interest is his pay-packet. The accent on money is understandable – after all, we are shorter of it than most. In a factory basic wage rates are usually low. Not that management can't afford to pay more: indeed, they do pay more – but not on the basic rate. Those last few £s that bring one a little nearer the elusive 'national average wage' have to be earned under pressure. By incentive schemes, piecework, bonus, merit-pay, call it what you will, the worker is introduced to the spirit of free enterprise competition. A wage to be earned becomes a prize to be won. Payment by results they call it. And the result of the result is yet another rise in the profits.

It is possible, of course, to achieve an increase in pay through promotion. However, factory workers who attain higher status appear to do so as much by their outlook as their ability. Working-class Tories (there are more of them than many people think – and though they don't outnumber the Socialists, they are more voluble) are far more destined for glory than their Left-wing workmates. The system of promotion is hard to define; it's not so much preference as a rather subtle form of natural selection. Anyway, satisfaction with one's lot and acceptance of authority are considered by management to be more important than skill. Under our present system of industrial control this may be advantageous. But restriction of free expression, at all levels, is greatly to blame for the lack-lustre reputation of British industry. Management, and to a certain extent the unions, have no time for the nonconformist. Neither, for that matter, has society.

I help to make cigarettes. I also smoke them – I'm smoking one now. Each employee of the firm for which I work receives, from the age of 18, a free issue of cigarettes weekly. Initiation by gift. Personally, I'd prefer the money to the fringe-benefit, but it's the cigarettes or nothing. Admitted, I could sell the cigarettes, but I don't. So I smoke; even though I agree with the medical profession about the relationship between smoking and lung-cancer. Sometimes I feel as if I'm living in an arsenal, an arsenal full of noisy machines painted green – the colour of grass – attended by green-overalled women. My workmates know little and care less about the lung-cancer side of smoking. It's a long way from the tobacco factory to the coffin. So we keep churning them out, millions a day, converting the rather attractive raw material, parchment-like tobacco leaf, into unattractive cigarettes. We make a pittance, the company makes a fortune. Other drug pedlars go to prison.

It would be wrong to assume, however, that factory workers helping to produce more worthwhile things than cigarettes find their jobs any more satisfying. They don't, and they admit it. The end-product provides no consolation to anyone who works in a factory. It is the factories, not what is made, that makes factory workers what they are. There is something about factory life that is inconsistent with man's progress through time; something retrograde. It is as if one is going down the other side of the evolutionary hill.

Factories may differ, but those working in them are all suffering from the same industrial malaise. We are all second fiddles to machines.

It gets worse, too. Complicated new machinery doesn't make the worker's job any more rewarding: the effect is the opposite. Less, rather than more, skill is required. As machines grow more complex so they become more self-reliant. They need less looking after; and they get it. As automation increases productivity it also provides management with an excuse to cut down on labour. At first the workers object to a reduction in their numbers, but nearly always they eventually acquiesce; as things stand, they haven't much choice. So where one saw a man looking vacantly at two machines one now sees him looking just as vacantly at six. This may be a greater strain on his eyes, but it certainly doesn't give him any more responsibility or food for thought.

Though men are in charge of the machines, the actual operation of them is usually done by women. Sometimes there are as many as five women to a machine. In some departments the proportion of women to men is immense: yet supervision remains the prerogative of the male. The suffragettes didn't have much effect on the factory. The women are more talkative than the men; their topics differ, too. Where the men tend to moan about pay and conditions (but won't do anything about them), the women chatter all day long about their homes, their holidays, who's in the family-way and anything else unconnected with work. Women turn their minds from the futility of factory life. Maybe they are wise. Anyway, they are much happier than the men, and more independent. They are much more likely to ask for their cards. I'd ask for mine if I was a woman with a husband at work.

The factory at which I work overlooks a cemetery. Beyond the cemetery rows of sooty houses stretch to the horizon. The prospect from the factory window reminds me of a concentration camp. And yet this is where we live: this is where we are expected to find recompense for the pound of flesh we sell to industry. One might find it necessary to work in prison, but one should not be required to live in one.

Inside the factory the prospect is just as grim. To me, anyway, though the others seem not to notice it. The workers, that is. For management, of course, are ever willing to help in the division of labour. They recognize two categories of employee: staff and worker. It is more the type of job than the importance of the work that decides one's category. To work in an office is the passport to the élite. Although we are all employed by the same firm, the staff get more money, more pension, more sick-pay, more holidays, and work shorter hours, than the workers. The supervisor and the clerk are segregated from the mechanic by pay and conditions of work. The segregation is not without the moral overtones that have become connected with the word. Staff implies status. And how some people love position. White collars are worn like halos, and the words 'I'm on the staff' spoken as a self-reference.

(Passage by Dennis Johnson from *Work: 1*, ed. R. Fraser, 1968)

1. According to the author, the factory workers get no satisfaction from their work. Why, then, do they do it?

2. Explain the relationship that the author sees between machinery and lack of job satisfaction.

3. What are the differences in the roles of men and women in the factory? Who do you think gets paid the least?

4. What are the main differences between 'staff' and 'workers'?

5. The factory worker is described as someone who has *no control* over the production process. The work he or she does is *meaningless* to the worker. The worker has no opportunity to use his or her individual skill or creativity and therefore has *no self-satisfaction*. Work is only *a means to an end*: work only allows the possibility of achieving rewards outside the factory gates. In general, the worker is said by sociologists to be 'alienated' from his work. Do you think that school pupils are often 'alienated'? Use the four ideas in italics above and apply them to the situation of a typical pupil.

6. Write an essay of 300 words on ways of reducing alienation in work.

5C TRADE UNIONS

Union membership in the UK

(a) Men and Women

| | Millions | | As a Percentage of all Employees | |
	Men	Women	Men	Women
1961	7·9	2·0	53	24
1978	9·3	3·8	65	38

(b) Selected Trade Unions

| | Thousands | |
	1961	1978
National Union of Mineworkers	675	371
National Union of Railwaymen	317	197
Iron and Steel Trades Confederation	125	113
Union of Shop, Distributive, and Allied Workers	351	462
Civil and Public Servants Association	143	225
Confederation of Health Service Employees	58	215

1. Who are most likely to belong to a trade union: (a) men (b) women?

2. The number of women belonging to trade unions has nearly doubled between 1961 and 1978. Does this mean that working women are nearly twice as likely to belong to a union in 1978 compared with 1961?

3. What changes have occurred in the membership of the first three and the last three unions in Table (b)?

4. Give reasons for the changes referred to in Question 3 (for one of the main reasons, you might find it helpful to look back at Exercise 5A in this Chapter).

5. What are the main functions of trade unions?

5D STRIKES

This chart shows the strike record in the United Kingdom compared with that of other countries, in terms of working days lost through industrial stoppages per thousand employees. The figures include both official and unofficial strikes and lock-outs, and are based on data collated by the International Labour Office (ILO). They relate primarily to the mining, manufacturing, construction, and transport industries since the ILO consider that this basis provides the best comparison between the countries.

The data are derived from national data which are collected according to different methods and concepts. In particular, although most countries exclude small stoppages, the thresholds differ between countries in terms of the number of workers involved or the duration before a stoppage is officially recorded. However, the effects of such differences are not likely to be substantial in terms of the number of working days lost. A recent study of industrial stoppages in the United Kingdom showed that on average five industries – coal mining, docks, motor vehicle manufacturing, shipbuilding, and iron and steel – accounted for a quarter of strikes and a third of working days lost, although they only cover about six per cent of employees. In the first half of 1979 working days lost through strikes were more than double the same period in 1978, with nearly five times as many workers involved.

Industrial disputes: international comparison

Average number of working days lost per thousand employees (Mining, manufacturing, construction, and transport industries)

¹ Manufacturing only.   ³ All sectors included up to 1971.   ⁴ Including gas, electricity, and water.
² 1968 excluded from average.   1977 excluded from average.

Source: Department of Employment Gazette.

(From *Social Trends* 10, 1980)

1. Construct two international 'league tables' (one for 1968–72 and one for 1973–77) based on the chart above. The country with the highest number of working days lost per 1,000 employees should be at the top of each table and the country with the fewest working days lost at the bottom.

2. The UK's international reputation as a strike-prone nation is such that commentators refer to the 'English disease' of industrial disputes. Looking at your 'league tables', would you say that this reputation is entirely justified?

3. According to the introductory passage, 6% of employees in the UK were involved in ——% of all strikes and ——% of all working days lost. (Fill in the blanks.)

4. The passage lists five strike-prone industries in the UK. Give reasons why these industries are more affected by industrial disputes than others.

5. What effects might industrial stoppages in these five industries have on the nation?

6. List some of the causes of industrial disputes.

7. Strikes are only one measure of industrial discontent. What are some of the others?

5E LEISURE

Participation rates" for selected leisure activities by sex, and, for males, by age and socio-economic group 1977

Great Britain

percentages

	Playing football	Darts	Watching football	DIY/ house repairs	Cinema	Dancing	Betting/ pools	Records/ tapes
Males	6	15	7	51	11	14	29	64
Females	–	4	1	22	10	16	11	60
Males								
Aged 16–19	24	31	12	32	29	29	8	93
20–24	17	33	10	48	28	25	23	87
25–29	10	27	10	59	18	16	30	81
30–44	5	17	8	63	10	15	33	73
45–49	–	9	6	55	5	14	35	59
60+	–	3	4	35	2	4	26	34
Socio-economic group								
Professional	6	10	9	67	14	14	15	73
Employers/ managers	3	9	7	58	9	16	23	67
Intermediate non-manual	7	11	9	64	13	12	23	74
Junior non-manual	7	12	7	52	13	14	28	65
Skilled manual/own account non-professional	6	18	8	51	10	15	34	62
Semi-skilled manual/ personal service	4	16	7	42	9	12	34	59
Unskilled	3	15	3	35	8	10	30	46

* In the four weeks prior to interview (annual average)

(From *Population Trends* 17, Autumn 1979)

1. Discuss the participation rates for men and women as presented in the table.

2. What appears to be the relationship between the age of a male and the likelihood that he will gamble?

3. What pattern is apparent in the participation by different socio-economic groups in DIY/House repairs? Is this pattern in any way surprising?

4. All of the leisure activities mentioned in the table are actually work for some people. Give three examples of these.

5. What distinguishes work from leisure?

6. Why might some groups in an industrial society like Britain 'need' leisure?

6 POPULATION

6A   DEFINITIONS

Give clear definitions of the following terms used in demography (the study of population). Many of these terms are used in later questions in this chapter:

Birth Rate	Migration	Sex Distribution
Death Rate	Immigration	Dependent Population
Natural Increase	Emigration	Working Population
Infant Mortality	Net Migration	Dependency Ratio
Expectation of Life	Age Distribution	

6B   POPULATION CHANGES IN THE UK

Population changes and projections

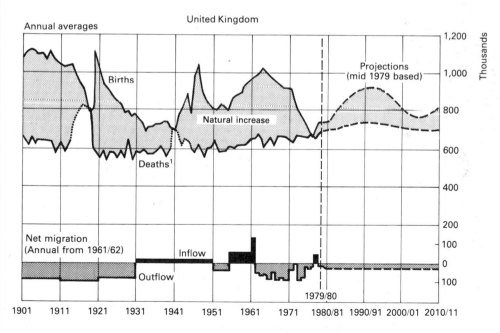

[1] The dots on this line cover the periods 1914–18 and 1939–45 which include deaths of non-civilians and merchant seamen who died outside the country.

Source: Office of Population Censuses and Surveys

(From *Social Trends* 11, 1981)

1. Give a detailed description and explanation of the changes in births, deaths and net migration as depicted in the chart above.

2. Give at least one reason why the number of births is likely to increase again in the 1980s and early 1990s.

3. Explain why a graph of birth and death *rates* for the UK over the same period (1901–1979/80) would look different from the graph on p. 39.

6C POPULATION CHANGES IN DIFFERENT COUNTRIES

Country	Population (Millions)	Birth Rate	Death Rate	Infant Mortality	Life Expectancy Males	Females
UK	55·5	11·8	11·7	14·0	67·8	73·8
USA	203·3	15·3	8·8	14·0	68·7	76·5
India	548·2	35·2	15·9	122·0	41·9	40·6
Uganda	9·5	45·2	15·9	160·0	48·3	51·7
W. Germany	60·7	9·5	11·5	15·5	68·3	74·8
Chile	8·9	23·9	7·8	55·6	60·5	66·0

(Adapted from *United Nations Statistical Yearbook*, 1978)

1. In which country in the above table is the population increasing at the fastest *rate*?

2. In which country is the population increasing by the greatest *number*?

3. In what way is the population change in West Germany going to be different from that of the other countries in the table?

4. Explain how Chile can have a lower death rate than the USA or UK despite having a higher infant mortality rate and a lower life expectancy than these two countries.

5. What are the social and economic consequences of rapid population growth?

6D POPULATION BY AGE AND SEX

Population by age and sex, England and Wales

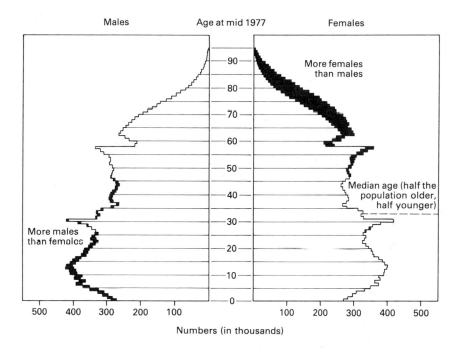

Males   Age at mid 1977   Females

(From *Population Trends* 15, Spring 1979)

1. The shading in the chart shows where the number of males exceeds the number of females and vice versa. At what age do the females begin to outnumber the males?

2. What past event has affected the number of males aged over 75 in 1977?

3. What other non-biological factors might account for the shorter life expectancy of males compared to females in England and Wales?

4. Why are there unusually *low* numbers of people aged 58–62 and 35–45 and unusually *high* numbers of people aged 55–58 and 28–31?

5. Looking at people aged under 30, at which age are there the fewest people? What strikes you about your answer?

6. If the majority of people convicted of criminal offences are aged between 14 and 21, what change might you expect in the criminal statistics for 1992 compared to those for earlier years?

7. What are the social and economic problems associated with: (a) 'bulges' and 'troughs' in the age structure of the population and (b) the increasing proportion of people beyond retirement age?

8. Find your own 1977 age-group on the chart. What advantages or disadvantages have there been in the past and might there be in the future for you and your age-group compared to other age-groups born 5–10 years before or after you were?

6E   MIGRATION WITHIN THE UK

Average annual net migration 1971 to 1978

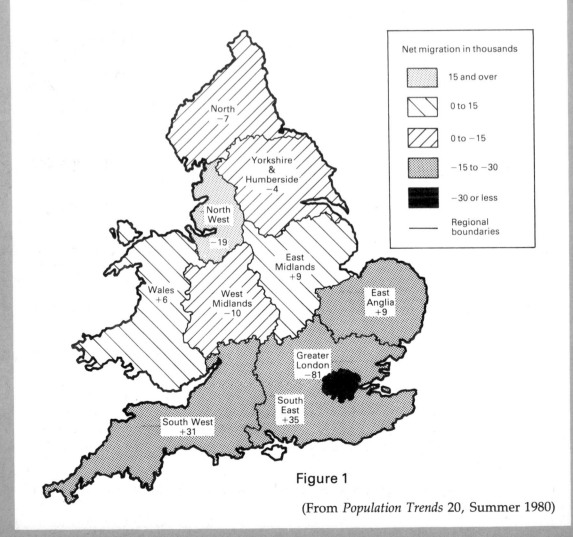

Figure 1

(From *Population Trends* 20, Summer 1980)

Population change, age-groups, England and Wales 1971–77

Figure 2

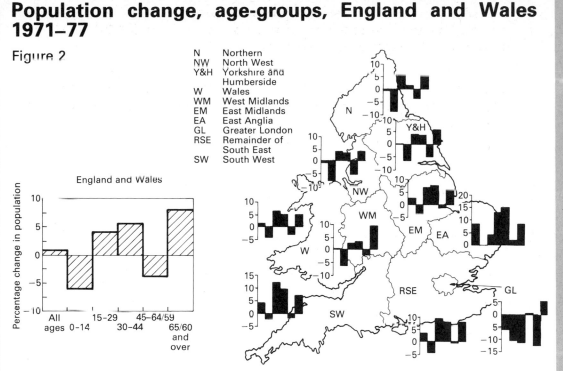

(From *Population Trends* 16, Summer 1979)

1. Looking at Figure 1, which region has the highest net *gain* in migration between 1971 and 1978?

2. In Figure 1, what pattern can be observed in the older industrial areas of England and Wales?

3. Looking at the large graph for England and Wales in Figure 2, account for the percentage increases and decreases in different age groups between 1971 and 1978. (You may find the graph in Exercise IV useful here.)

4. Looking at both Figures 1 and 2, summarise the changes that have taken place in Greater London between 1971 and 1977/78.

5. In Figure 2, how does East Anglia differ from all the other regions in its population change?

6. In Figure 2, you will notice that the population (all ages) in the West Midlands has increased very slightly despite the fact that Figure 1 shows that the West Midlands lost 10,000 people through migration during the same period. What other factors are affecting population change in that region?

7. Give reasons why the population in England and Wales moves from one region to another.

The Background

Geriatrica is a Western industrialised society in the early 1990s. It has a population of 50 million and a land area similar to that of France. Its industrial production has become increasingly automated through the use of microprocessors and robots, although there are many areas of production (agriculture, luxury consumer goods, etc.) that have not yet adopted such technological advances. Nearly 60% of the workforce are employed in the tertiary or service sector of the economy. The economy is reasonably stable, having recovered from the recession of the early 1980s.

The unemployment rate is about 10%, many of the unemployed being over 45 years of age (the over-45s suffered most from the effects of recession and of automation in industry in the 1980s). In addition, there is a growing number of people aged over 50 who have taken early retirement and are living on company or civil service pensions. The increasing life expectancy in Geriatrica means a continuing expansion in the proportion of over-65s.

This increasing proportion of older people who are no longer working is a growing problem for the government. Firstly, expenditure (pensions, medical and social services, etc.) on the older population has increased rapidly. Secondly, the over-45s are now a sizeable percentage of the electorate. Politically it is becoming harder to resist demands for higher pensions and better social services.

At the other end of the age spectrum, there has been a rapid increase in the birth rate as those mothers born in the 'baby boom' of the 1960s have babies themselves. Although it is believed that the birth rate will fall by 1995/96, this 'bulge' will soon be working its way through the education system, requiring increased expenditure on teachers and facilities. It is also likely that these children will stay in education longer than those of a decade earlier because the increasingly technological nature of Geriatrica require higher levels of knowledge in its workforce.

In short, Geriatrica faces a serious dependency problem: increasing numbers of unemployed or retired over-45s, a high unemployment rate and an increase in the number of dependent schoolchildren. There is grave concern in government circles over whether the economy will be able to support this large dependent population.

The Problem

You are a senior minister in the government of Geriatrica. You and your colleagues learn that two government-financed Medical Research Institutes have simultaneously made major breakthroughs in medical treatment, one in heart disease and the other in cancer.

It is estimated that these two breakthroughs are likely to extend the lives of people over 45 by an average of ten years. The new treatments would be appropriate for tens of thousands of patients per year, the cancer treatment costing an average of £9,000 per patient and the heart treatment an average of £10,000 per patient. The state medical system would have to bear these costs.

This apparently good news is scheduled to be announced in one week's time. Therefore, you and your fellow government ministers have only a few days to consider the social, political and economic consequences of these medical advances and to decide on government policy (whether official or unofficial).

Write a 500-word paper for the Prime Minister of Geriatrica on what the consequences might be and on what possible decisions the government could make.

7 SOCIAL CONTROL

7A PARENTAL CONTROL

Four-year-old children: Parental control by social class

	Social Class I+II	III (Non-Man)	III (Man)	IV	V
	%	%	%	%	%
1. Proportion of children bedwetting at least occasionally.	14	22	31	27	30
2. Child allowed by mother to see both parents unclothed.	59	45	27	24	15
3. Mothers would not yet tell child where babies come from.	12	27	55	47	75
4. Obedience, if refused, enforced by smacking.	56	63	70	63	79
5. Child smacked for lies.	27	37	38	44	42
6. Child smacked for trying to smack his mother.	43	50	63	60	64
7. Child smacked for temper tantrums.	20	33	36	38	25
8. Idle threats of authority figure.	6	17	23	26	39
9. Deprivation (sweets, etc.).	60	77	69	72	67
10. Child voluntarily confesses to misbehaviour.	65	54	54	44	31

(Adapted from *Four Years Old in an Urban Community* by J and E Newsom, 1970)

1. According to the table, in which five aspects of parental control are the differences between Classes I + II and Class V the most pronounced?
2. What is the most common reason in all social classes for smacking a child?
3. Looking at the table, which group of children are generally more likely to be smacked by their parents:
   (a) working class
   (b) middle-class
4. What conclusions *might* you come to by comparing items 5 and 10 in the table?
5. In primitive societies, particularly those in warm climates, toilet training is not an important problem. However, in Western industrialised societies toilet training is a major preoccupation. Why might this be so?
6. What other biological functions of children and young people are socially controlled by adults?

REWARDS AND INCENTIVES AT SCHOOL ━━━

Reward or incentive	Least effective ⟵━━━━━━⟶ Most effective
Success in a test	
Good marks for written work	
Election to position of authority by teacher	
Election to position of leadership by fellow pupils	
Given a prize	
Public praise	
Favourable report for home	
Given marks for team or house in class work	
Temporary leadership in games	
Score success for team or house in sports	
Going with form on some outing	
Quiet appreciation from teacher	

Key:

────── Schoolboys' (11–15 years old) opinions of the effectiveness of rewards or incentives.

╴╴╴ Teachers' opinions of the effectiveness of rewards or incentives.

(Adapted from NFER Report *A Survey of Rewards and Punishments in Schools*, 1952)

1. Compare the teachers' and pupils' opinions of the effectiveness of various rewards and incentives. What does this comparison reveal?

2. Give some reasons for the opinions of both pupils and teachers.

3. What implications does this information have for the effectiveness of the teachers' control over their pupils?

4. This table is concerned with rewards. What punishments or sanctions can teachers also use?

5. Teachers can use very subtle rewards or punishments in the classroom. What are some of these?

6. What control, if any, do pupils have over their teacher or teachers?

7C   AUTHORITY AND OBEDIENCE

In this extract from Norman Mailer's *The Naked and the Dead*, a novel about American GIs in World War II, General Cummings is worried about the decline in his troops' discipline and respect for him. In particular, he is enraged when he returns to his tent to find that one of his junior officers, Lieutenant Hearn, has deliberately stubbed out a cigarette on the floor despite knowing that this would annoy the General:

> . . . what Hearn had done was equivalent to a soldier's laying hands on his person. To Cummings it was a symbol of the independence of his troops, their resistance to him. The fear, the respect his soldiers held for him now was a rational one, an admission of his power to punish them, and that was not enough. The other kind of fear was lacking, the unreasoning one in which his powers were immense and it was effectively a variety of sacrilege to thwart him. The cigarette butt on the floor was a threat, a denial of him, as fully as Lanning's defection, or a Japanese attack on his lines, and he had to meet it directly and ruthlessly. The longer you tarried with resistance the greater it became. It had to be destroyed.
>
> Hearn looked at his watch. 'It's time to go to chow.' Outside the tent the earth was almost white in the glare of the overhead sun.
>
> 'You'll go to chow when I release you.'
>
> 'Yes, sir.' Hearn scraped his foot slowly against the floor, stared at him quietly, a little doubtfully.
>
> 'You threw that cigarette on my floor today, didn't you?'
>
> Hearn smiled. 'I figured that was going to be the point of all this talk.'
>
> 'It was simple enough for you, wasn't it? You resented some of my

actions, and you indulged a childish tantrum. But it's the kind of thing I don't care to permit.' The General held his half-smoked cigarette in his hand, and waved it slightly as he spoke. 'If I throw this down on the floor, would you pick it up?'

'I think I'd tell you to go to hell.'

'I wonder. I've indulged you too long. You really can't believe I'm serious, can you? Supposed you understood that if you didn't pick it up, I would court-martial you, and you might have five years in a prison stockade.'

'I wonder if you have the power for that?'

'I do. It would cause me a lot of difficulty, your court-martial would be reviewed, and after the war there might be a *bit* of a stink, it might even hurt me personally, but I would be upheld. I would have to be upheld. Even if you won eventually, you would be in prison for a year or two at least while it was all being decided.'

'Don't you think that's a bit steep?'

'It's tremendously steep, it has to be. There was the old myth of divine intervention. You blasphemed, and a lightning bolt struck you. That was a little steep too. If punishment is at all proportionate to the offense, then power becomes watered. The only way you generate the proper attitude of awe and obedience is through immense and disproportionate power. With this in mind, how do you think you would react?'

Hearn was kneading his thighs again. 'I resent this. It's an unfair proposition. You're settling a difference between us by . . .'

'You remember when I gave that lecture about the man with the gun?'

'Yes.'

'It's not an accident that I have this power. Nor is it that you're in a situation like this. If you'd been more aware, you wouldn't have thrown down that cigarette. Indeed, you wouldn't have if I were a blustering profane General of the conventional variety. You don't quite believe I'm serious, that's all.'

'Perhaps I don't.'

Cummings tossed his cigarette at Hearn's feet. 'All right, Robert, suppose you pick it up,' he said quietly.

There was a long pause. Under his breastbone, Cummings could feel his heart grinding painfully. 'I hope, Robert, that you pick it up. For your sake.' Once more he stared into Hearn's eye.

And slowly Hearn was realizing that he meant it. It was apparent in his expression. A series of emotions, subtle and conflicting, flowed behind the surface of his face. 'If you want to play games,' he said. For the first time Cummings could remember his voice was unsteady. After a moment or two, Hearn bent down, picked up the cigarette, and dropped it in an ashtray. Cummings forced himself to face the hatred in Hearn's eyes. He was feeling an immense relief.

'If you want to, you can go to chow now.'

'General, I'd like to transfer to another division.' Hearn was lighting another cigarette, his hands not completely steady.

'Suppose I don't care to arrange it?' Cummings was calm, almost cheerful. He leaned back in his chair, and tapped his foot slowly. 'Frankly, I don't particularly care to have you around as my aide any longer. You aren't ready to appreciate this lesson yet. I think I'm going to send you to the salt mines. Suppose after lunch you report over to Dalleson's section, and work under him for a while.'

'Yes, sir.' Hearn's face had become expressionless again. He started toward the exit of the tent, and then paused. 'General?'

'Yes?' Now that it was over, Cummings wished that Hearn would leave. The victory was losing its edge, and minor regrets, delicate little reservations, were cloying him.

'Short of bringing in every man in the outfit, all six thousand of them, and letting them pick up your cigarettes, how are you going to impress them?'

This was the thing that had sullied his pleasure. Cummings realized it now. There was still the other problem, the large one. 'I'll manage that, Lieutenant. I think you'd better worry about your own concerns.'

After Hearn had gone, Cummings looked at his hands. 'When there are little surges of resistance, it merely calls for more power to be directed downward.' And that hadn't worked with the line troops. Hearn he had been able to crush, any single man he could manage, but the sum of them was different still, resisted him still. He exhaled his breath, feeling a little weary. There was going to be a way, he would find it. There had been a time when Hearn had resisted him too.

1. Where does General Cummings' authority come from? Is it from:
   (a) customs and tradition,
   (b) his personality,
   (c) his position in the organisation (i.e. the army)?

2. Soldiers in most armies find it easy to tell what job other soldiers in that army do and to tell who has authority over whom. They can do this even if the other soldiers are complete strangers. What distinctive feature of most armies makes this possible?

3. How does General Cummings control Lieutenant Hearn? Is it through:
   (a) coercion (the use or threat of physical force or punishment),
   (b) incentives (money, food, promotion, etc.),
   (c) shared interests or shared ideas about behaviour (politeness, self-help, loyalty, bravery, team spirit, etc.)?

4. What problems does the General face in controlling the rest of his soldiers?

5. Which of the three types of control listed in Question 3 are used in the following organisations:
   (a) a car factory,
   (b) a prisoner-of-war camp,
   (c) a social club,
   (d) a school?

Shooting an Elephant

by George Orwell

In Moulmein, in Lower Burma, I was hated by large numbers of people – the only time in my life that I have been important enough for this to happen to me. I was sub-divisional police officer of the town, and in an aimless, petty kind of way anti-European feeling was very bitter. No one had the guts to raise a riot, but if a European woman went through the bazaars alone somebody would probably spit betel juice over her dress. As a police officer I was an obvious target and was baited whenever it seemed safe to do so. When a nimble Burman tripped me up on the football field and the referee (another Burman) looked the other way, the crowd yelled with hideous laughter. This happened more than once. In the end the sneering yellow faces of young men that met me everywhere, the insults hooted after me when I was at a safe distance, got badly on my nerves. The young Buddhist priests were the worst of all. There were several thousands of them in the town and none of them seemed to have anything to do except stand on street corners and jeer at Europeans.

All this was perplexing and upsetting. For at that time I had already made up my mind that imperialism was an evil thing and the sooner I chucked up my job and got out of it the better. Theoretically – and secretly, of course – I was all for the Burmese and all against their oppressors, the British. As for the job I was doing, I hated it more bitterly than I can perhaps make clear. In a job like that you see the dirty work of Empire at close quarters. The wretched prisoners huddling in the stinking cages of the lock-ups, the grey, cowed faces of the long-term convicts, the scarred buttocks of the men who had been flogged with bamboos – all these oppressed me with an intolerable sense of guilt. But I could get nothing into perspective. I was young and ill-educated and I had had to think out my problems in the utter silence that is imposed on every Englishman in the East. I did not even know that the British Empire is dying, still less did I know that it is a great deal better than the younger empires that are going to supplant it. All I knew was that I was stuck between my hatred of the empire I served and my rage against the evil-spirited little beasts who tried to make my job impossible. With one part of my mind I thought of the British Raj as an unbreakable tyranny, as something clamped down, *in saecula saeculorum*, upon the will of prostrate peoples; with another part I thought that the greatest joy in the world would be to drive a bayonet into a Buddhist priest's guts. Feelings like these are the normal by-products of imperialism: ask any Anglo-Indian official, if you can catch him off duty.

One day something happened which in a roundabout way was enlightening. It was a tiny incident in itself, but it gave me a better glimpse than I had had before of the real nature of imperialism – the real motives for which despotic governments act. Early one morning the sub-inspector at a police station the other end of the town rang me up on the phone and said that an elephant was ravaging the bazaar. Would I please come and do something about it? I did not know what I could do, but I wanted to see what was happening and I got on to a pony and started out. I took my rifle, an old .44 Winchester and much too small to kill an elephant, but I thought the noise might be useful *in terrorem.* Various Burmans stopped me on the way and told me about the elephant's doings. It was not, of course, a wild elephant, but a tame one which had gone 'must'. It had been chained up as tame elephants always are when their attack of 'must' is due, but on the previous night it had broken its chain and escaped. Its mahout, the only person who could manage it when it was in that state, had set out in pursuit, but he had taken the wrong direction and was now twelve hours' journey away, and in the morning the elephant suddenly reappeared in the town. The Burmese population had no weapons and were quite helpless against it. It had already destroyed somebody's bamboo hut, killed a cow and raided some fruit-stalls and devoured the stock; also it had met the municipal rubbish van, and, when the driver jumped out and took to his heels, had turned the van over and inflicted violence upon it.

The Burmese sub-inspector and some Indian constables were waiting for me in the quarter where the elephant had been seen. It was a very poor quarter, a labyrinth of squalid bamboo huts, thatched with palm-leaf, winding all over a steep hillside. I remember that it was a cloudy stuffy morning at the beginning of the rains. We began questioning the people as to where the elephant had gone, and, as usual, failed to get any definite information. That is invariably the case in the East; a story always sounds clear enough at a distance, but the nearer you get to the scene of events the vaguer it becomes. Some of the people said that the elephant had gone in one direction, some said that he had gone in another, some professed not even to have heard of any elephant. I had almost made up my mind that the whole story was a pack of lies, when we heard yells a little distance away. There was a loud, scandalized cry of 'Go away, child! Go away this instant!' and an old woman with a switch in her hand came round the corner of a hut, violently shooing away a crowd of naked children. Some more women followed, clicking their tongues and exclaiming; evidently there was something there that the children ought not to have seen. I rounded the hut and saw a man's dead body sprawling in the mud. He was an Indian, a black Dravidian coolie, almost naked, and he could not have been dead many minutes. The people said that the elephant had come suddenly upon him round the corner of the hut, caught him with its trunk, put its foot on his back and ground him into the earth. This was the rainy season and the ground was soft, and his face had scored a trench a foot deep and a couple of yards long. He was lying on his belly with arms crucified and head sharply twisted to one side. His face was coated with mud, the eyes wide open, the teeth bared and grinning with an expression of unendurable agony. (Never tell me, by the way, that the dead look peaceful. Most of the corpses I have seen looked devilish.) The friction of the great beast's foot had stripped the skin from his back as neatly as one skins a rabbit. As soon as I saw the dead man I sent an orderly to a friend's house near by to borrow an elephant rifle. I had already sent back the pony, not wanting it to go mad with fright and throw me if it smelled the elephant.

The orderly came back in a few minutes with a rifle and five cartridges, and meanwhile some Burmans had arrived and told us that the elephant was in the paddy fields below, only a few hundred yards away. As I started forward practically the whole population of the quarter flocked out of their houses and followed me. They had seen the rifle and were all shouting excitedly that I was going to shoot the elephant. They had not shown much interest in the elephant when he was merely ravaging their homes, but it was different now that he was going to be shot. It was bit of fun to them, as it would be to an English crowd; besides, they wanted the meat. It made me vaguely uneasy. I had no intention of shooting the elephant – I had merely sent for the rifle to defend myself if necessary – and it is always unnerving to have a crowd following you. I marched down the hill, looking and feeling a fool, with the rifle over my shoulder and an ever-growing army of people jostling at my heels. At the bottom when you got away from the huts there was a metalled road and beyond that a miry waste of paddy fields a thousand yards across, not yet ploughed but soggy from the first rains and dotted with coarse grass. The elephant was standing eighty yards from the road, his left side towards us. He took not the slightest notice of the crowd's approach. He was tearing up bunches of grass, beating them against his knees to clean them and stuffing them into his mouth.

I had halted on the road. As soon as I saw the elephant I knew with perfect certainty that I ought not to shoot him. It is a serious matter to shoot a working elephant – it is comparable to destroying a huge and costly piece of machinery – and obviously one ought not to do it if it can possibly be avoided. And at that distance, peacefully eating, the elephant looked no more dangerous than a cow. I thought then and I think now that his attack of 'must' was already passing off; in which case he would merely wander harmlessly about until the mahout came back and caught him. Moreover, I did not in the least want to shoot him. I decided that I would watch him for a little while to make sure that he did not turn savage again, and then go home.

But at that moment I glanced round at the crowd that had followed me. It was an immense crowd, two thousand at the least and growing every minute. It blocked the road for a long distance on either side. I looked at the sea of yellow faces above the garish clothes – faces all happy and excited over this bit of fun, all certain that the elephant was going to be shot. They were watching me as they would watch a conjurer about to perform a trick. They did not like me, but with the magical rifle in my hands I was momentarily worth watching. And suddenly I realized that I should have to shoot the elephant after all. The people expected it of me and I had got to do it; I could feel their two thousand wills pressing me forward, irresistibly. And it was at this moment, as I stood with the rifle in my hands, that I first grasped the hollowness, the futility of the white man's dominion in the East. Here was I, the white man with his gun, standing in front of the unarmed native crowd – seemingly the leading actor of the piece; but in reality I was only an absurd puppet pushed to and fro by the will of those yellow faces behind. I perceived in this moment that when the white man turns tyrant it is his own freedom that he destroys. He becomes a sort of hollow, posing dummy, the conventionalized figure of a sahib. For it is the condition of his rule that he shall spend his life in trying to impress the 'natives' and so in every crisis he has got to do what the 'natives' expect of him. He wears a mask, and his face grows to fit it. I had got to shoot the elephant. I had committed myself to doing it when I sent for the rifle. A sahib has got to act like a sahib; he has got to appear resolute, to know his own mind and do definite things. To come all that way, rifle in hand, with two thousand people marching at my heels, and then to trail feebly away, having done nothing – no, that was impossible. The crowd would laugh at me. And my whole life, every white man's life in the East, was one long struggle not to be laughed at.

But I did not want to shoot the elephant. I watched him beating his bunch of grass against his knees, with that pre-occupied grandmotherly air that elephants have. It seemed to me that it would be murder to shoot him. At that age I was not squeamish about killing animals, but I had never shot an elephant and never wanted to. (Somehow it always seems worse to kill a *large* animal.) Besides, there was the beast's owner to be considered. Alive, the elephant was worth at least a hundred pounds; dead, he would only be worth the value of his tusks – five pounds, possibly. But I had got to act quickly. I turned to some experienced-looking Burmans who had been there when we arrived, and asked them how the elephant had been behaving. They all said the same thing: he took no notice of you if you left him alone, but he might charge if you went too close to him.

It was perfectly clear to me what I ought to do. I ought to walk up to within, say, twenty-five yards of the elephant and test his behaviour. If he charged I could shoot, if he took no notice of me it would be safe to leave him until the mahout came back. But also I knew that I was going to do no such thing. I was a poor shot with a rifle and the ground was soft mud into which one would sink at every step. If the elephant charged and I missed him, I should have about as much chance as a toad under a steam-roller. But even then I was not thinking particularly of my own skin, only the watchful yellow faces behind. For at that moment, with the crowd watching me, I was not afraid in the ordinary sense, as I would have been if I had been alone. A white man mustn't be frightened in front of 'natives'; and so, in general, he isn't frightened. The sole thought in my mind was that if anything went wrong those two thousand Burmans would see me pursued, caught, trampled on and reduced to a grinning corpse like that Indian up the hill. And if that happened it was quite probable that some of them would laugh. That would never do. There was only one alternative. I shoved the cartridges into the magazine and lay down on the road to get a better aim.

The crowd grew very still, and a deep, low, happy sigh, as of people who see the theatre curtain go up at last, breathed from innumerable throats. They were going to have their bit of fun after all. The rifle was a beautiful German thing with crosshair sights. I did not then know that in shooting an elephant one should shoot to cut an imaginary bar running from ear-hole to ear-hole. I ought therefore, as the elephant was sideways on, to have aimed straight at his ear-hole; actually I aimed several inches in front of this, thinking the brain would be further forward.

When I pulled the trigger I did not hear the bang or feel the kick – one never does when a shot goes home – but I heard the devilish roar of glee that went up from the crowd. In that instant, in too short a time, one would have thought, even for the bullet to get there, a mysterious, terrible change had come over the elephant. He neither stirred nor fell, but every line of his body had altered. He looked suddenly stricken, shrunken, immensely old, as though the frightful impact of the bullet had paralysed him without knocking him down. At last, after what seemed a long time – it might have been five seconds, I dare say – he sagged flabbily to his knees. His mouth slobbered. An enormous senility seemed to have settled upon him. One could have imagined him thousands of years old. I fired again into the same spot. At the second shot he did not collapse but climbed with desperate slowness to his feet and stood weakly upright, with legs sagging and head drooping. I fired a third time. That was the shot that did it for him. You could see the agony of it jolt his whole body and knock the last remnant of strength from his legs. But in falling he seemed for a moment to rise, for as his hind legs collapsed beneath him he seemed to tower upwards like a huge rock toppling, his trunk reaching skyward like a tree. He trumpeted, for the first and only time. And then down he came, his belly towards me, with a crash that seemed to shake the ground even where I lay.

I got up. The Burmans were already racing past me across the mud. It was obvious that the elephant would never rise again, but he was not dead. He was breathing very rhythmically with long rattling gasps, his great mound of a side painfully rising and falling. His mouth was wide open – I could see far down into caverns of pale pink throat. I waited a long time for him to die, but his breathing did not weaken. Finally I fired my two remaining shots into the spot where I thought his heart must be. The thick blood welled out of him like red velvet, but still he did not die. His body did not even jerk when the shots hit him, the tortured breathing continued without pause. He was dying, very slowly and in great agony, but in some world remote from me where not even a bullet could damage him further. I felt that I had got to put an end to that dreadful noise. It seemed dreadful to see the great beast lying there, powerless to move and yet powerless to die, and not even to be able to finish him. I sent back for my small rifle and poured shot after shot into his heart and down his throat. They seemed to make no impression. The tortured gasps continued as steadily as the ticking of a clock.

In the end I could not stand it any longer and went away. I heard later that it took him half an hour to die. Burmans were arriving with dahs and baskets even before I left, and I was told they had stripped his body almost to the bones by the afternoon.

Afterwards, of course, there were endless discussions about the shooting of the elephant. The owner was furious, but he was only an Indian and could do nothing. Besides, legally I had done the right thing, for a mad elephant has to be killed, like a mad dog, if its owner fails to control it. Among the Europeans opinion was divided. The older men said I was right, the younger men said it was a damn shame to shoot an elephant for killing a coolie, because an elephant was worth more than any damn Coringhee coolie. And afterwards I was very glad that the coolie had been killed; it put me legally in the right and it gave me sufficient pretext for shooting the elephant. I often wondered whether any of the others grasped that I had done it solely to avoid looking a fool.

1. Why did the Burmese hate the Europeans, particularly the British?

2. What is meant by 'imperialism'? What does 'tryanny' mean?

3. Give two reasons why Orwell found his role of policeman difficult.

4. Describe the differences and similarities between his role as a policeman in Burma and that of a policeman in Britain now.

5. In about 100 words, give a sociological explanation of the factors that led Orwell to shoot the elephant despite the fact that he says that 'I did not in the least want to shoot him.'

6. In his description, Orwell uses a number of images to do with acting and the theatre. Give examples of some of these.

7. 'All the world's a stage.' How far can social behaviour be compared to a drama in a theatre?

8. Give two examples of social situations in which an individual's behaviour is influenced by the expectations of other people.

Manchester: Police prosecutions for male importuning

1955	1
1956	0
1957	0
1958	2
1959	30
1960	105
1961	135
1962	216

(**Source:** *The Police* by Ben Whitaker, 1964)

I. By what *proportion* has the number of prosecutions in the above table increased between 1958 and 1962?

2. At the end of 1958, a new Chief Constable took over in Manchester. Does this fact in any way affect how you interpret the figures in the table? Give reasons for your answer.

3. Using the table, what can you say, if anything, about the *actual* amount of male importuning in Manchester between 1955 and 1962?

4. Give at least three *sociological* reasons why the police might concentrate on certain kinds of crime or certain groups of people rather than others. Give examples.

5. Suppose a local council mounted an 'anti-vandalism campaign', encouraging local residents to report acts of vandalism to the police. What effect might this have on the local crime statistics compared to those for earlier years?

6. The police are agents of social control (i.e. they control social behaviour). Name at least three other agents or agencies of social control.

8 DEVIANCE

8A   PHYSICAL DEVIANCE

While the term 'deviance' is usually used with reference to differences in social behaviour, physical differences can also be socially important. The following extract comes from the autobiography of a cripple:

> I also learned that the cripple must be careful not to act differently from what people expect him to do. Above all they expect the cripple to be crippled; to be disabled and helpless: to be inferior to themselves, and they will become suspicious and insecure if the cripple falls short of these expectations. It is rather strange, but the cripple has to play the part of the cripple, just as many women have to be what the men expect them to be, just women; and the Negroes often have to act like clowns in front of the 'superior' white race, so that the white man shall not be frightened by his black brother.
>
> I once knew a dwarf who was a very pathetic example of this indeed. She was very small, about four feet tall, and she was extremely well educated. In front of people, however, she was very careful not to be anything other than 'the dwarf', and she played the part of the fool with the same mocking laughter and the same quick, funny movements that have been the characteristics of fools ever since the royal courts of the Middle Ages. Only when she was among friends, she could throw away her cap and bells and dare to be the woman she really was: intelligent, sad and very lonely.
>
> But people do not only expect you to play your part; they also expect you to know your place. I remember for instance a man at an open-air restaurant in Oslo. He was much disabled, and he had left his wheel-chair to ascend a rather steep staircase up to the terrace where the tables were. Because he could not use his legs he had to crawl on his knees, and as he began to ascend the stairs in this unconventional way, the waiters rushed to meet him, not to help, but to tell him that they could not serve a man like him at that restaurant, as people visited it to enjoy themselves and have a good time, not to be depressed by the sight of cripples.

(From *And Yet We Are Human* by Finn Carling, 1962)

1. Explain what the author means by saying that cripples are expected '. . . to be inferior to themselves.'

2. '. . . many women have to be what the men expect them to be, just women.' What do you think this means? Give examples.

3. Why should people be '. . . depressed by the sight of cripples' (last paragraph)?

4. People who may be regarded as being physically different (cripples, the blind, the dark-skinned, etc.) often refuse to accept that they are socially

inferior. What are some of the ways in which they might try to convince others that they are 'normal' human beings?

5. Some people get upset by the unorthodox dress or appearance of either men or women (long-haired men, 'unisex' clothing, women in coarse work clothing, etc.). Why might such people be disturbed by the confusions caused?

8B   SKINHEADS

Skinheads: the cult of trouble

The image is white convict. **Ian Walker** talked to skinheads about their world.

Skinheads streaming out of Camden Town underground tonight look hard and they know it. The crop is the style, but it can also be the weapon: it'll nut you if you look too long or you don't step out of the way, if you're wearing the wrong uniform or follow the wrong team. Outside the Electric Ballroom four Special Patrol Group men stand staring at the line of skinheads waiting to pay £3.00 to see UB40, staring at the anti-fashion parade.

The smart look is sta-prest trousers, Ben Sherman shirts and polished Dr Martens. The tougher look is a short-sleeved shirt displaying the tattoos, bleached Levis with the braces hanging loose round the legs. The real hard cases have tattoos on their faces. One has a small cross on each cheek. Most of the girl skins look really young, about 13, and are dressed like the boys in shirts, jeans and boots. But some wear short skirts, like one black skinhead girl who's got brown monkey boots over black fishnet tights.

The police point and giggle at all the girls in miniskirts. Now and again they try to show who the real tough guys are by frogmarching the odd skinhead to the back of the queue.

Skins: the image is white convict, the music is black. (Remember Norman Mailer's article on the cult of hip, 'The white Negro'?) Groups like UB40—the name comes from the DHSS code for the unemployed—are now called two-tone because they put black and white musicians together to play ska, an early form of reggae coming out of Jamaica, and popular with the first wave of British skinheads in the 1960s.

It is not just skinheads who are into two-tone. Punks, Rastas, rude boys (skins in mohair suits), and a few long hairs, are here too. But inside the Electric Ballroom, this huge and airless hall, it's the skinheads who make the atmosphere charged ... There's a loud crack and heads turn. But it's just a skin who's finished his can of Coke and smashed it on the floor.

A skinhead tries to make an art form out of *machismo*. He walks, chin out military style, with a duck-splayed swagger. He sucks hard on his cigarette, chews his gum with a vengeance. He doesn't smile too much, unless he's with his mates at the bar. The only time a skin looks somehow vulnerable is when he's dancing—never with a girl, always either alone or with other skins—with his eyes half-closed, dipping his shoulders rhythmically. Skinheads are great dancers.

'It's just fashion, innit?' says a 16 year old from south London, watching his mate zap the Space Invaders in the bar, rocking, gently to the reggae of Reality, the warm-up band. Two girls—one has MINISKIN N4 DODGER painted on the back of her army-green jacket—run full-tilt through the bar, scant regard for drink or bodies. Skin girls, aim to be as street-tough as the boys. They strut to the front of the queue at the women's toilets. No one complains.

Although skin boys don't hang out with skin girls, every now and again a boy will just waltz up to a girl, kiss her violently for a couple of minutes, before moving off wordlessly ... These boys, with their POW haircuts and markings, their enamel Union Jack badges, their polished boots—these boys don't get too upset if they're taken for fascists. Fascism is a laugh.

A boy in a red Fred Perry tennis shirt greets his friend with a Nazi salute, grinning. Another skinhead wandering round the bar has WHITE POWER written in blue on his T-shirt. A black roadie for UB40 stops and scowls at him, but the white supremacist ignores the challenge, walks on by.

At 10.30, UB40 come on stage and there's a rush from the bars as the skins make for the front of the hall. Two Rastafarians and six whites in this band. 'This is one of our Rock Against Thatcher numbers,' says the frontman. A few half-hearted cheers. 'Are there only 50 people here into Rock Against Thatcher?' He gets a bigger cheer. A drunk skinhead staggers through the packed dance floor, trying to kick the guy running away from him, before giving up the chase and collapsing on the floor. Everyone ignores him. Be cool.

The final encore over, the lights come on, and the plastic pint pots are ceremoniously crunched. West Ham skins sing 'Wembley' (pronounced Wemballee) on their way out, throwing down the gauntlet to the Arsenal.

It's not picked up. It's been a quiet night, after all. Police are back on duty outside as the dancers spill out, dripping with sweat this warm night, and traipse down the street for the underground train home. Home to their parents, most of them, though there is one last pleasure to be squeezed out the night: to chant and sing and look tough on the tube. Scaring the straights is half the fun.

It always has been. Seat-slashing Teds, mass-rioting mods and rockers, football thugs, skinheads, drug-taking hippies, foul-mouthed punks ... Sub-editors write headlines, politicians fire moralism from the hip, youth movements come and go.

Skinhead first arrived in the late 1960s. It was a sort of male working class backlash against the mods grown too narcissistic, effeminate and arty. Football fans discovered a style. I remember 4,000 Manchester United skinheads on the terraces at Elland Road, in Leeds in 1968. They all wore bleached Levis, Dr Martens, a short scarf tied cravat-style, cropped hair. They looked like an army and, after the game, went into action like one. (I also remember that the first time I went to the Electric Ballroom, to see a skinhead band, I ended up over the back of a red sports car on Camden High Street. A skinhead told me there was no room upstairs on the 253. He was lying. I went upstairs ... That was in 1978.)

Skinheads never really disappeared from the football terraces. But the clothes, like skinhead music (soul, ska, home-grown rabble-rousers like Slade), went out of fashion, until the punk movement turned style inside out, starting in late 1976. A new generation of skins started following the band called Sham '69. 'If punks are about anarchy, then skinheads are the most anarchist going,' Jimmy Pursey, the band's frontman, told me.

(From *New Society*, 26 June 1980)

1. Skinheads say they are anti-fashion. Does the description in paragraph two bear this out?

2. Why might a name like 'UB40' seem appropriate for a band playing to the kind of audience described (paragraphs 4 and 5)?

3. What attitudes, behaviour and fashions might lead skinheads to be '... taken for fascists'?

4. 'Scaring the straights is half the fun. It always has been. Seat-slashing Teds, mass-rioting mods and rockers, football thugs, skinheads, drug-taking hippies, foul-mouthed punks ...' Why might youth movements tend to rebel against the 'straight' world?

5. '... youth movements come and go.' What happens to the majority of rebellious teenagers as they grow older?

6. Skinheads and punks were both reactions against the 'commercialisation' of youth culture (fashions, music, etc.). Explain what 'commercialisation' means here.

Violent Britain myth or reality?

A spate of vicious and apparently senseless street assaults; a set of alarming crime figures issued by Scotland Yard. The impression that Britain is becoming a more violent society has gained rapid ground in the past few weeks. But is that really the case? PHILLIP KNIGHTLEY and MARJORIE WALLACE look behind the statistics to report on what the figures actually reveal, and on the real trends they may be concealing.

It is 11.30 at night, and the casualty department at University College Hospital, London, is relatively quiet—it is a Tuesday and the evening has so far been free of major incidents. Suddenly there is activity. Police arrive with an 18-year-old youth, John, who is holding a cloth to an open gash in his forehead. His white tee-shirt is spattered with blood.

As hospital staff tend to his wound, John, a sturdily built young man, but badly shaken, explains what happened. He had, he says, been walking with a friend along a street in Mount Pleasant, when they were accosted by 20 boys aged between 14 and 16.

'They were tooled up to the top—sticks, iron bars, broken glass, nails,' John says. 'They got us on the ground and started kicking us. I heard them grunting and shouting "Get 'em, kill 'em". They were trying to outdo each other. I felt a blow on the side of my head an then I was too dazed to notice much else.

'Looking back on it what amazes me is the age of them, the size of them. They must all have been still at school. In my day we did it all with fists, one to one. Now these kids pick on the first person they see. There's no reason for it. They do it for a laugh. They were really loving it.'

John's experience was no surprise to the staff in the casualty department. Last week there were 19 similar cases: an elderly woman beaten up in a shop, a girl attacked in a new estate by men with razors, an old man mugged and robbed, a young man slashed on the face in the street. Two Sundays ago there were six assaults in seven hours.

The staff there are convinced that the incidents they see suggest

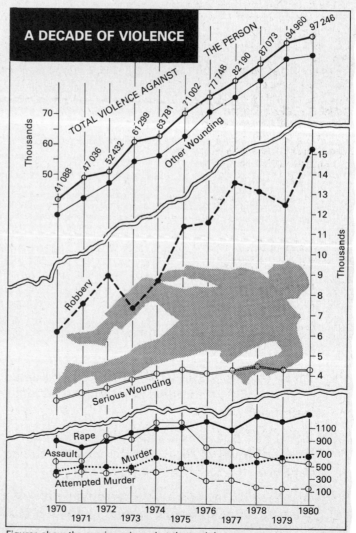

A DECADE OF VIOLENCE

Figures show the soaring crime—but the truth is more complex

a sharp increase in the rate of 'random' violence—assaults at the hands of an unknown assailant, either for robbery or for some unexplained motive. 'It's violence for violence's sake,' said the casualty night sister. But the UCH is only one hospital in London, and London only one city in Britain. Is there any objective evidence that the country as a whole reflects that picture?

The obvious place to start is the Home Office, which publishes each year criminal statistics for England and Wales (Scotland publishes its own). These summarise serious offences reported to or witnessed by the police, and list various categories of violent crimes. At first glance the figures appear to confirm a trend of escalating violence. The murder rate, for example, appears to have risen, over the past ten years, by 57 per cent; 'wounding endangering life' has gone up by 48 per cent; and 'other wounding' by an astounding 153 per cent.

But drawing firm conclusions from these statistics is fraught with pitfalls. The number of murders in 1980—620—turns out to have been inflated by a large number of deaths associated with fires started deliberately. In March and August two London fires killed 47 people, pushing up the murder rate substantially. In Hull 23 people died in nine fires between 1973–78, but these were not recorded by the police as murder until 1980, and so did not enter the homicide statistics until then.

Even if no allowance at all is made for these 'freak' figures, the number of homicides recorded in 1980 is actually *below* the peak figure for the past 10 years—629 in 1979—and the murder rate in London itself is down on 1979 by two per cent. Furthermore, the chances of being murdered by an outsider rather than family or friends is still low and has remained so since 1972.

Wounding and endangering life, although showing an increase over a 10-year period, is actually down on 1979 and on 1978. Attempted murder is down considerably over a 10-year period (340 cases in 1970, 155 last year) and has shown a steady decline since a peak in 1975 (499 cases). The number of cases of assault has increased only slightly over a 10-year period (531 to 557) and the trend since 1975 is steadily downwards.

Rape reports have increased 38 per cent over ten years. But the anonymity given to victims in court reporting since 1976 has encouraged more women to go to the police, which has altered the figures. Even so, the number of reports in 1980 (1,225) is only slightly up on 1979 and below that of 1978.

To sum up: if we rely on the Home Office statistics, the number of offences of violence against the person recorded in 1980 was only a fraction higher than in 1979, whereas the average annual increase over the previous ten years was ten per cent. It is just possible, then, that 1980 saw the start of a *slowing down* of violence in Britain.

That still leaves within this all-embracing 'violence against the person' category, the enormous increase in other wounding, 35,779 in 1970 to 90,654 in 1980. The Home Office offers no statistical explanation or theory for this rise. The figures are unlikely to have been affected by changes in the counting rules introduced on January 1, 1980 and can probably be considered to represent a genuine change in the level of offences actually recorded.

Here one has to confront the indefinable effect of 'fashions' in reporting crime. One theory is that today's citizens are more likely to report offences to the police than their parents were because they are conditioned to expecting the authorities to handle society's problems. Another belief is that whenever newspapers or television concentrate on a certain type of crime, like 'mugging', there is an increase in the number of people reporting it. And this fashion may well be reflected by the reporting officer who is ultimately responsible for which category a crime is listed under. So the figures may be a better reflection of the way officialdom records crime today than of society itself.

The Home Office does not break down its 'other wounding' figures in the same way as it does its murder totals—into 'victim acquainted with the suspect' and 'victim not acquainted with the suspect'. So we cannot conclude how many of those 90,654 victims of other woundings suffered at the hands of their relatives, lovers, friends or acquaintances rather than being victims of 'random violence'.

(From *The Sunday Times*, 21 June 1981)

1. At first glance, the illustration looks like a single graph for all the crimes described. How many sets of graphs are actually contained within the one illustration?

2. At the top is a graph with a line plotting 'Total Violence Against the Person'. Which of the other crimes on the graphs are *included* in this category?

3. According to the extract, it is difficult to discover what these criminal statistics really represent. Explain in about 300 of your own words why it is so hard to find out the true extent of crime in Britain.

The table below shows the ages and sexes of offenders found guilty of, or cautioned for, indictable/triable either-way offences. An offender who is 'cautioned' is not formally charged but is 'let off' with a severe warning from a senior police officer.

'Indictable' offences are the more serious forms of lawbreaking (e.g. not having a current TV licence is a non-indictable offence). 'Triable either-way' offences are those that can be tried in either a Magistrates Court or a Crown Court.

Offenders found guilty of, or cautioned for, indictable/triable either-way offences: by age, sex, and type of offence, 1979

	England & Wales											Percentages
	Males: age ranges				All ages		Females: age ranges				All ages	
	10 to 13	14 to 16	17 to 20	21 and over	(per-cent-ages)	(thous-ands)	10 to 13	14 to 16	17 to 20	21 and over	(per-cent-ages)	(thous-ands)
England & Wales												
Indictable/triable either-way offences:												
Murder, manslaughter, or infanticide	0·3	3·4	21·1	75·2	100	0·4	–	1·5	14·9	83·6	100	0·1
Other violence against the person	3·1	14·0	28·8	54·1	100	47·9	6·0	25·7	19·4	48·9	100	4·8
Sexual offences	3·7	15·9	19·9	60·6	100	10·1	8·9	9·6	18·5	63·0	100	0·1
Burglary	16·1	30·2	24·9	28·7	100	66·1	23·4	32·2	22·8	21·6	100	3·0
Robbery	5·9	17·9	34·7	41·5	100	3·1	8·4	33·7	33·2	24·7	100	0·2
Theft and handling stolen goods	14·5	22·9	22·0	40·6	100	222·5	17·5	19·7	13·7	49·1	100	73·0
Fraud and forgery	2·0	5·7	18·3	74·0	100	17·1	2·2	7·8	24·3	65·7	100	5·0
Criminal damage	17·9	22·1	27·3	32·7	100	10·5	15·3	21·6	16·6	46·5	100	0·8
Other indictable/ triable either-way (excluding motoring) offences	0·3	2·4	19·9	77·4	100	19·7	0·3	3·8	22·7	73·2	100	2·6
Triable either-way motoring offences	0·4	8·7	21·9	69·0	100	21·0	0·3	6·3	12·2	81·3	100	0.7
Total indictable/ triable either-way offences	11·3	20·4	23·1	45·1	100	418·3	15·5	19·3	15·2	50·0	100	90·4
Number of offenders per 1,000 population in age group	29	68	62	12		20	9	15	9	3		4

Source: Criminal Statistics, *Home Office, Scottish Home and Health Department*

(From *Social Trends* 11, 1981)

1. What are the three most common offences for (a) males and (b) females?

2. Which age-group has the highest rate of offenders among (a) males and (b) females?

3. What is the overall ratio of males to females in the table?

4. Write about 300 words on why male offenders far exceed females in this table.

9 RACE RELATIONS

Many people in Britain claim that the colour of a man and women's skin is unimportant and that it is the 'foreign' habits and culture of coloured 'immigrants' that cause prejudice and discrimination. If these immigrants were as 'British' as the existing white population, discrimination would therefore disappear.

But what if a white Englishman were suddenly to turn brown? The following extract describes an interesting example:

> ... If they ask what difference the prejudice of white English people would make to their personal lives if their skin turned brown, they may like to reflect on the case of a Welshman, an ex-commando and former Services boxing champion, living in a Dorset town. He suffered from a kidney disease which meant that he had to seek lighter work. The disease also darkened his skin so that he was mistaken for a coloured man (Humphrey and John, 1971: 20–21). As a result he has experienced colour prejudice. 'It is not as if it happened just once. It might happen 10 times a week. I have known it to happen three times a day. Sometimes I have been stopped in the street by a stranger, who says something like: "You bloody wog, why don't you go back to the palm trees?"' He applied for work as a sales representative or insurance salesman only to learn (when they saw his face) that employers thought colour a bar: 'because I look like a Pakistani I cannot get a job' (*Guardian*, 24 July 1970). Two days later it was reported by the *Observer* that 'he is no longer to lose his home after all—although he can no longer keep up his mortgage repayments. His local council is to buy his house and rent it back to him at a rate he can afford ... The local Lions Club has bought him a refrigerator, and paid for a course of driving lessons to help him get a job as a driver. He has been allowed to fall behind with his rates and electricity bills.'

(From *Racial Minorities* by Michael Barton, 1972)

1. What is the difference between 'prejudice' and 'discrimination'?

2. What does this passage tell us about the importance of skin colour for prejudice?

3. The man described in the passage received assistance in a number of ways. Is this the kind of assistance also generally given to 'real' Pakistanis? Give an explanation for your answer.

4. People are often surprised to hear a West Indian or an Asian talking with a strong Scouse, Cockney or Brummie accent. Account for this surprise.

5. Some white people go out of their way to be especially talkative and friendly to coloured people whom they meet at work, at parties and so on. Does this mean that they are not colour prejudiced?

The first post-war black immigrants arrived from the West Indies in June 1948: on a ship called the *Empire Windrush*. The 492 on board, mostly men from Jamaica, were a happy and high-spirited group. Many of them were ex-servicemen of the RAF. During World War Two about 7,000 West Indians had enlisted for the RAF and had been stationed in the United Kingdom. They had returned home after the war, but now they were looking forward with high hopes to good jobs in England.

West Indians

Commonwealth immigrants from the West Indies were attracted to Britain mainly because they knew there were jobs waiting for them here. They may not have wanted to leave their homeland, but regular well-paid jobs were very scarce in their own countries. It was especially difficult for returning ex-servicemen to find good jobs.

After the war Britain suffered an acute shortage of labour, especially in semi-skilled jobs. Everywhere new homes, schools, roads and hospitals were being built, to make up for bomb damage and the slowdown of construction during the war. New social services were introduced, including the National Health Service. The factories began to make peace-time goods and they found the labour shortage particularly serious. A Government Department was set up to recruit foreign workers from Europe. Between 1945 and 1957, more than 350,000 Europeans helped to reduce the labour shortage.

Meanwhile West Indians, too, were given information about job vacancies in Britain. In the island of Barbados, London Transport set up an office to recruit workers in 1956, soon to be followed by the Hotels and Restaurants Association and the National Health Service, which encouraged girls to come over to nurse in British hospitals. In 1954 about 9,000 West Indians came to Britain. By 1956 the figure had jumped to nearly 30,000, showing the success of the British employers' recruitment drives. Numbers fell again, only to reach a new peak of over 66,000 in 1961. This increase in numbers probably resulted from attempts to 'beat the ban' of the Immigration Act of 1962, which West Indians were expecting. Public discussion in the British newspapers and in Parliament made it clear that very soon controls on New Commonwealth immigration were to be introduced.

These were some of the factors which 'pulled' West Indians to Britain. At first many of the immigrants probably intended to save up and return to their homeland. But when it became clear that work prospects back home were not improving, more and more decided to stay. They began to save up to bring over their children and other close relatives. 'Dependants'—that is, wives and children under sixteen—did not need work vouchers to enter Britain. As the number of work vouchers declined, the number of dependants entering went up. In 1967, the total of dependants immigrating from *all* New Commonwealth countries was over 50,000. Here, then, was another 'pull' factor—dependants coming not for work but to join their families. They continued to enter in controlled numbers into the 1970s.

Another factor which explains why Jamaicans especially, chose to come to Britain is that they were prevented from emigrating to the USA. A law passed in 1952 restricted their entry to that country to a mere 100 a year. Ever since about 1910 thousands of Jamaicans had settled in the USA. It was much nearer than Europe and therefore cheaper to travel there. But after 1952 West Indians turned their eyes to Britain.

(From *Race Relations in Britain*, by Mercia Last, 1978)

1. What pressures encouraged West Indians to leave their own countries?

2. Why did the British encourage West Indians to come to Britain?

3. In which year did the largest number of West Indians come to Britain?

4. Britain was the 'second choice' for many West Indians. Where was their 'first choice' and why couldn't they choose it?

5. The passage deals with why West Indians came to Britain. However, by the late 1970s there were more people of West Indian extraction going to the West Indies than there were coming to Britain (i.e. a net loss in migration). Give at least two reasons why this was happening.

9C   HOUSING FOR IMMIGRANTS

There are dramatic differences between the minority groups and the rest of the population in terms of housing tenure and the quality of housing occupied, and there is still more fundamental contrast in the relation between these two things. Among the general population, owner-occupation and good-quality housing are strongly associated: the more affluent people are, the higher their standard of housing, and the more likely they are to be owner-occupiers. Among the minority groups, as we shall see, none of these connections holds good.

Table I.   Tenure – West Indians, Asians and the general population

	West Indians	Asians	General population†
	%	%	%
Owner-occupied	50	76	50
Rented from council	26	4	28
Privately rented	24	19	22
Not stated	1	1	*

† *Source:* 1971 census – households in England and Wales.

Table II. Type, age and external condition of dwelling – summary comparison between minorities and whites

	Minorities	Whites
Type of dwelling:	%	%
Detached	1	21
Semi-detached	15	36
Terraced	66	30
Flat/rooms/maisonette	15	12
Not stated	3	1
Age of dwelling:		
Built before 1914	46	24
Built before 1940†	86	48
External condition of dwelling:		
Very good	28	55
Very good or average†	58	89

† Includes previous category.

Table III. Households with 2 or more persons per bedroom

West Indians	Asians	Whites†
34%	41%	11%

† The comparison survey includes households with male heads only.

Table IV. Households *not* having exclusive use of bath, hot water and inside WC

West Indians	Paki-stanis/ Bangla-deshis	Indians	African Asians	General population
%	%	%	%	%
33	57	35	31	17·9‡

‡ This figure is from the 1971 census.

(Adapted from *Racial Disadvantage in Britain* by David J Smith, 1977)

1. Tables I and IV refer to the 'General Population' while Tables II and III refer to 'Whites'. What is the difference between these two categories?

2. Re-read the introductory passage. Explain the last sentence with reference to *Asian* groups, using relevant information in the tables.

3. What type, age and condition is the majority of the housing of the minority groups?

4. What percentages of the following groups live in housing built *since* 1940: (a) minorities, (b) whites?

5. What reasons can you give for the generally inferior housing of minority groups?

I

Many of the Asian immigrants will be oriented towards their home communities. They will be saving money in order to return and be more concerned to maintain a good reputation in their home village than among the English.

Many Asians will have many relatives around them ... For such reasons the lives of the Asian immigrants are influenced in important ways by the expectations of the homeland culture ... The West Indians, on the other hand, do not seek to maintain a distinctive homeland culture. They are not involved in such tight community and kinship networks as the Asians ... In the early years especially, many West Indian immigrants regarded England as their mother country and were willing to conform to British expectations if in this way they could gain social acceptance.

(From *Racial Minorities* by Michael Banton, 1972)

II

A.K. comes from Campbellpore, where he worked on the family farm, six years ago. He has worked for short periods in Bradford, Sheffield, Cardiff, and Smethwick but left all these jobs as he objected to paying bribes to avoid the dirtiest and heaviest jobs. He now lives with his brother in Sparkbrook and works at a motor-car factory where he says there is no bribery. He does not much like English workers but thinks his present Managing Director is a 'good man'. A.K. speaks very poor English and seldom goes out. He spends a lot of time reading his Qoran and is deeply religious (which his brother takes as a sign of his mental simplicity). When we first met A.K., he was sitting in his room playing a small harmonium-like instrument and singing to himself. He is quite happy in England now, but yearns for his wife. He will not bring her to England as he believes it would be impossible to maintain Purdah* here. It would not be good for his wife to see English ways (kissing in public). England is a morally corrupt country with thousands of divorces to prove it. A.K. was deeply shocked to learn that one of us was nearly thirty years old and unmarried. He firmly believes in early, arranged marriages, preferably at about the age of sixteen. He thinks he will return to Pakistan 'some day', but he is not sure when. Meanwhile, he lives in a room with the kitchen attached, acting as manager for his brother who owns the house and lets it to West Indian and Irish lodgers. A.K. does his own cooking and cooks for his brother (who also has a flat and a café in Aston) when the brother is in.
(Pakistani, Birmingham, 1964)

* 'Purdah' – being secluded and kept from meeting men
(From *Race, Community and Conflict* by J Rex and R Moore, 1967)

III

Over the tea Mark says he has no time for mods ('just a load of wimps'), Teds, rockabillies or Asians. Why Asians? 'I don't like Pakis and I don't know any skinheads who do. Pakis just don't mix. You'll see one of them,' he points to the Peter Toch* poster, 'with a white man. Never see a Paki with one. Paki-bashing is all part of the cult anyway.'

There is an Asian band in south London called Alien Kulture who take gangs of Asian youth with them wherever they play. Mark had said he thought 'niggers are okay, I like the music'. But he just shakes his head about Alien Kulture: 'I don't think they'll last. I don't think they'll last five minutes. A Paki band? I never heard of such a thing.'
(Skinhead, London, 1980)

---

* West Indian Reggae star

(From *New Society*, 26 June 1980)

1. In extract **I**, West Indian and Asian attitudes towards the British way of life are contrasted. Summarise these differences.

2. Do you think that the last sentence of extract **I**, still holds true for many West Indians?

3. Mr A.K. is probably more set in his ways than many Pakistanis in England. Find at least five reasons in extract **II** why Mr A.K. is unlikely to fit easily into white English society.

4. In many societies (USA, South Africa, etc.) racial tension rises when coloured groups attempt to mix with the white society. How does this contrast with the skinhead's reasons for disliking Pakistanis (extract **III**)?

5. Why might an Asian band deliberately call themselves 'Alien Kulture'?

In 1980, rioting broke out in the St Paul's district of Bristol, following incidents involving mainly black youths and the police.

In April 1981, several days of violent rioting occurred in Brixton, London (see the chapter on Mass Media for newspaper headlines reporting the riots).

Three months later, rioting occurred in many of Britain's urban areas. In Southall, London, Asians retaliated against skinhead provocation and assault. In Toxteth, Liverpool, there were violent clashes between youths (white and black) and the police. In Moss Side, Manchester, there were several nights of disturbances. In Brixton tempers flared after a police raid resulted in extensive damage to private property.

The following article from *The Guardian* newspaper examines some of the factors that may have contributed to the first eruption of hostility in Brixton in April, 1981.

BRIXTON'S MORNING AFTER: As the debris was cleared yesterday, two writers walked and talked in the riot area. Mike Phillips is a West Indian journalist.

SUNDAY morning around Railton Road was like carnival time. The mood of the local residents and spectators out walking in the area of Brixton devasted by Saturday night's riots was cheerful, and oddly proud. 'This,' said one youth I spoke to, 'was the black man's Christmas.'

This was a reaction which was typical of many of the youths who had been involved in the events of the weekend and it stems from a number of factors to do with the anger and frustration felt throughout the black community in Britain and particularly in Brixton.

Herman Ouseley, Community Liaison Officer for Brixton, yesterday refused to locate the problem merely in the events of the last two weeks. 'When Bristol happened, everyone was saying, Brixton next. We were living in anticipation, in a way, of exactly this happening; and everyone said, when it happens it will be a lot bigger than Bristol.'

There are obvious reasons. First, the background. Lambeth, the South London borough where Brixton is situated had, for instance, an

ambitious plan for housing in the area. 'But we've seen plans come and we've seen plans go.' At the moment there are 18,000 people on the waiting list for housing. Registered unemployment is expected to rocket to something like 2,000 later in the year. Most of the registered umemployed are black—'two out of three'.

Lambeth has 1,500 places on training schemes, larger than any other borough. 'But what happens when they finish their six months on the Youth Opportunity Schemes? They're out again, a little more experienced, but still out of work.'

The fact that black kids often don't register disguises the extent of the unemployment. 'I was at the neighbourhood project on Friday night,' Gabriel Solomon, a local community worker said, 'and one of the MSC men was around there talking to some kids, and they were giving him a hard time. By the time they've finished their schemes all that's left is cynicism.'

None of that is unusual. Brixton is a poor area. 'Over a third of the

housing stock is sub-standard.'

Over the last decade or more the district has been riddled with schemes, plans, community work projects, none of which could deliver the kind of material progress being demanded by black people in Brixton. Frustration is the word everyone uses.

'Previous Labour administrations,' says Ouseley, 'have ignored Brixton. Black people think it's because they're there. But Lewisham in comparison has several new shopping developments. Maybe it's the reputation of Brixton, I don't know, but there's been no improvement there for years. We had plans—we had a great new plan for housing in 1978, then the election and the curbs on public spending happened in 1979. We got left behind again.'

It's easy enough to deduce a lot of this from the look of Brixton. It's clearly an older district of London, with the sort of shops and firms which disappeared from North London high streets long ago. Up the side streets off Railton Road and Atlantic, there are attempts at improvement, especially in the odd houses where middle class folk have moved in and begun painting the front of the houses and cultivating the front gardens. Black people do all that too, but on any summer evening a walk down the central spine of the area, Frontline, is both stimulating and depressing.

Brixton is actually full of variety. For instance, there are projects set up by black groups and community workers to alleviate some of the problems which are thought to be characteristic of the place: Sabarr Bookshop (run by blacks), the Abeng Centre, the neighbourhood law centre. At the weekend there's a cheerful and excitable jostle of multi-racial crowds moving through the market, Cockney street trader chaff mingling with West Indian dialects. It can be a relaxed, friendly place.

In spite of all the problems, there's no racism on the streets, like there is in some areas. 'I suppose we have NF supporters here, but mostly they keep it to themselves.'

At the weekend an Asian drama group was performing at the Abeng Centre opposite the Brixton police station, the shoppers were moving around as usual, the youths and a lot of older folk were standing out in the spring sunshine. The sound systems were blasting out of the records shops. As far as the community itself was concerned everything was as usual, although tension had been winding up over the last two or three weeks. According to most residents, the police presence in the area had been escalating.

The police build-up was nothing new in Brixton. Early this year, Lambeth Council put out a report attacking the style and methods of policing there. The report repeated a number of the complaints familiar to anyone who's worked or lived in Brixton. Thus sus laws, under which police can gain conviction solely on the grounds of a reasonable suspicion that a person may be about to commit an offence. The stop and search methods of the Special Patrol Group, whose vans prowl the area, and who, have acquired a fearsome local reputation, and an all pervasive belief that the police see young blacks as an easy target for arrest or harassment.

Incidents, real or imagined, truthful or exaggerated, are relayed an amplified along Frontline with the speed of light. Everyone has a story which happened either to themselves or a relative or a friend. The police are the enemy and the implicit conflict between them and the young black people in the area isn't helped by the blandness of police denials, by the refusal of senior policemen to analyse the problem in the terms articulated by the Frontline folk.

Yesterday Metropolitan Police Commissioner Sir David McNee was hinting at the intervention of outsiders. 'Tell him,' a youth on the street said, 'to go back to Scotland. Him, don't know about London.'

In fact, the disturbances which occurred in Bristol a year ago ought to have given the police a sense of what would be the wrong style of conduct. The large scale police presence didn't cow the black youths. Instead it made them angry, and they responded in what one bystander described as 'the same macho style as the police'.

But there's still more to it all. The youths in Brixton are only part of an environment in which what happened on Saturday didn't horrify or surprise older and wiser black people. Senior community workers like Courtney Lawes, one of the black stalwarts of local race relations, were saying yesterday: 'This has been coming for twenty-five years. When we told them what would happen no one took any notice.'

A group of black local councillors meeting in London yesterday, called on the Home Secretary to act on 'the general political neglect of the racial dimension to the stresses and strains of Inner City life. Otherwise, such incidents will recur.'

That's a prediction that no one would argue with at this moment, especially in Brixton.

Michael Phillips

(From *The Guardian*, 13 April 1981)

1. What is the housing situation like in Brixton?

2. What are job and training prospects like for black youths in Brixton?

3. What criticisms are levelled at the police behaviour both before and during the riots?

4. The journalist who wrote the article is a West Indian. Does this affect your reading of the article? If it does, explain why.

5. Why are inner city districts often areas of poverty, bad housing and high concentrations of coloured minorities?

10 BELIEFS

10A   IN THE BEGINNING

Many peoples have stories or myths about the creation of their world. The Dinka are a tribe living in the Sudan in Africa.

> The Dinka believe that in the distant past the sky (where their god 'Divinity' lives) and the earth (where man lives) were once joined together. The sky lay just above the earth and men could move freely between the two by means of the rope that joined the sky and earth together.
>
> There was no death. The first man and woman were allowed only a single grain of millet per day, which was all they needed at the time.
>
> One day, the woman greedily decided to plant more than the single grain of millet that was allowed. As she hurriedly worked, she accidentally hit 'Divinity' with the handle of her hoe. 'Divinity' took great offence, cut the rope joining the sky and the earth and withdrew into the distance.
>
> As a result, man (i.e. the Dinka) were separated from their creator. They now suffer sickness and death. They now have to work for their food.

1. What do creation stories like this tell us about women?

2. Which sex is likely to be the dominant one in Dinka society?

3. What does the story imply about the reliability and reasonableness of 'Divinity'?

4. If 'heaven on earth' no longer exists because of (wo)man's folly, why do the Dinka bother to try to appease 'Divinity'?

5. The Dinka use religion to help explain the miseries that befall them. Give another example of a religion or belief system which does this.

6. Describe one example of a society in which religion helps to reinforce the social structure and to discourage social change.

10B   LUGBARA RELIGION

The Lugbara are a tribe living in the African country of Uganda. Like many other societies, the Lugbara have a number of myths which they pass on from one generation to the next. Many of these myths are about the origins of Lugbara society, while others concern the nature of other tribes in neighbouring areas.

These myths can be divided up into those dealing with time and those dealing with distance:

Time

Myths are told of the earliest ancestors, Jaki and Dribidu. These two 'hero-ancestors' were not human or social as Lugbara men are now. Dribidu means 'the hairy one' since his body was covered in long hair. These 'hero ancestors' did not live in a society and recognise its values. They behaved in the *reverse* manner to the way Lugbara live now. In this 'upside-down world' the 'hero ancestors' committed incest, ate their children, did not recognise ties of kinship, family or marriage, and could perform magical feats which men can no longer achieve.

As the time described gets nearer the present day, the myths gradually change their descriptions of the characters in them. The characters following the 'hero-ancestors' began to acquire some social and human characteristics. Nearer still to the present day and the people in the myths are presented as being 'normal' in Lugbara terms.

So the myths in time show a gradual progression from an 'upside-down world' to a 'normal' world.

Distance

The Lugbara also have myths about tribes in neighbouring areas.

Every Lugbara household sees itself as surrounded first by people like themselves. Then beyond the immediate community lies a circle of people whose territories are filled with sorcery and magic and who are evilly disposed toward the local Lugbara community.

People living in the far distance are believed to be beyond the bounds of society altogether: 'The most distant of these creatures, beyond the magicians and sorcerors, are thought to be hardly human in appearance. Although they are never visited, it is known that they walk on their heads. Peoples such as the Makaraka, the Momvu, the Mangbetu and ... the Azande are all reputed to be cannibals. They walk upside-down, beget children by their sisters, have terrible types of sorcery and live in thick forests in ways which the Lugbara cannot understand.' (John Middleton – *The Lugbara of Uganda*, 1965).

Once again the myths describe a gradual progression from a 'normal' world close-by to an 'upside-down' world off in the far distance, where people behave in the reverse manner to the Lugbara.

Summary

Thus the characters in Lugbara myths become stranger and stranger the further back in time or the further off in the distance they describe. The nearer one gets to the present time and place, the more normal these characters in the myths become.

Lugbara myths about time and distance

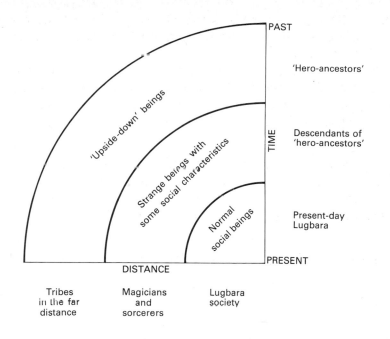

So the overall effect of these myths is to teach the Lugbara that things were very strange in the past and also that other societies are very strange.

1. What then do these myths tell the Lugbara about their own society at the present time?

2. Many societies tend to teach their members that they live in 'the best of all possible worlds at the best of all possible times'. Why?

3. Give reasons why we often refer to members of other societies as 'Yanks', 'Frogs', 'Wogs', 'Paddies', 'Krauts', 'Chinks', 'Niggers', 'Yids', etc.

4. The Lugbara describe other tribes as having strange characteristics. What exaggerated characteristics are sometimes associated with the groups mentioned in Question 3?

5. What school subjects tend to concentrate on aspects of our own society or land rather than on those of other societies?

6. Some people in this country believe that it is important to take pride in our nation whereas others feel that excessive national pride causes damage in the world as a whole. Give examples of some of the potentially good and bad aspects of nationalism (examples can include other societies as well as our own).

The following is part of a pamphlet distributed in American high schools in 1980/81 by the Ku Klux Klan:

A MESSAGE FROM THE IMPERIAL WIZARD ...

The Invisible Empire, Knights of the Ku Klux Klan is opening its ranks to young people between the ages of ten and seventeen. Membership into the KLAN YOUTH CORPS will help to mold young people into better citizens. Our program will help develop both mind and body of the nation's youth. The future of the United States and the western world will greatly depend on how our youth develop into adulthood.

An attempt is being made in our schools and universities to undermine the young people's respect for the values of our nation and our race. Black studies courses glorify mythological achievements of the black race. Christian values have been replaced by Jewish history and 'holocaust' study courses. Our nation's history has been reduced to that of a greedy colonial power, forcing lesser nations into subservience to our national whims. Jewish publishing houses have complete control over the editing, production and writing of our nation's textbooks.

Racial integration into the school systems has brought crime, drugs, forced sex, disease and general havoc to the classroom. The incidence of attacks against teachers has been given some notice by teachers groups and by the national media, but little notice is given to the violence against students by black savages who roam the corridors at will. Murder of white students by black students is on the increase. While murder is hard to hide in the nation's press, forced sex, robbery, forced drug use, and assault go unreported in the press.

It is time that the nation's white youth go on the offensive and organize to first protect themselves in the schools and secondly, to start an affirmative plan of action to build racial pride through a program of white racial courses. The history of the white race is one of great achievement in science, art, music, etc. The study of race should include the superior position of the white race. These are a few of the areas in which our nation's youth may participate to improve the quality of life through education.

Beyond the classroom and the school yard, the KLAN YOUTH CORPS will participate in voter registration drives, community improvement projects, social affairs and physical activities to build better and more healthful bodies.

The emphasis of the KLAN YOUTH CORPS will be on **quality**. We must constantly improve our capabilities through involvement. Membership in the KLAN YOUTH CORPS is the best answer to the problem of dropout mania. Without proper motivation, inspiration and rational programs, today's youth find if difficult to adjust in school, enter the job market, and generally enter the mainstream of society.

Aims and Objectives of the Klan Youth Corps

The Klan Youth Corps is an affiliate of the Invisible Empire Knights of the Ku Klux Klan (America's oldest, racialist fraternal order), and was founded on the same principles and traditions on which the Invisible Empire was founded over 100 years ago.

The Klan Youth Corps, like its parent group, recognizes that there are fundamental and biological differences between the White Race and the other races. It also recognizes that integration has been responsible for much of the racial strife in America, and most of the strife in our schools. Furthermore, the Klan Youth Corps is aware that integration is a prelude to miscegenation (race-mixing) which will lead to the down breeding of the White Race. It is therefore in the interest of the White Race and Western Civilization that racial separation of the races occur. From the humanitarian viewpoint, racial separation is desirable in that racial separation would guarantee the continued existence of all races; whereas, miscegenation would mean genocide and death for all races.

Racial separation, preferably through black repatriation to Africa, is the final and only desirable solution to America's racial problem in the opinion of the Klan Youth Corps and the Invisible Empire. Anything short of separation, will only add misery to an already agonizing situation. Of course, racial separation is still years off, and for that reason the Klan Youth Corps has developed a program that will allow it to address itself immediately to the racial problem in our schools, today, until racial separation is inacted.

KLAN YOUTH CORPS PROGRAM:

1) Organize White Youth in every school along racial lines.
2) 'Get tough' policy with arrogant non-Whites.
3) Force school administrators to drop their appeasement policy to minorities by threatening public exposure followed by possible boycotts.
4) Implement 'tit for tat' policy by demanding equal rights for White students. If minorities have a Minority Cultural Class. Whites should have a White Cultural Class (etc ...).
5) We want segregation of classes, followed by eventual segregation of schools.

THE FUTURE BELONGS TO US!

If you are proud of being white
If you are tired of black insults
If you want to improve yourself
If you have time to spare
If you are a person of action
If you are between ages 10 & 17

YOU BELONG IN THE KLAN YOUTH CORPS

APPLICATION BLANK ON REVERSE SIDE

---

1. In about 200 words, summarise *objectively* the beliefs and attitudes expressed in the pamphlet.

2. Explain in your own words the five points of the 'Klan Youth Corps Program'.

3. Publication and distribution of literature designed to 'incite racial hatred' is illegal in Britain. The Race Relations Acts of 1965, 1968 and 1976 have sought to restrict racial discrimination in most areas of life in Britain (employment, housing, education, advertising, etc.).
Legislation along similar lines was also passed in the mid-1970s to limit sexual discrimination.
Discuss the following statement: 'Laws against racial or sexual discrimination are a waste of time because Acts of Parliament cannot change people's basic beliefs and attitudes.'

10D   HOLY MATRIMONY? ▬▬▬▬▬▬▬▬▬▬

Percentage of Marriages in England and Wales that were Solemnised in Register Offices

1966	33
1971	41
1976	50
1979	51

1. According to the table, what is happening to the percentage of marriages solemnised by a religious ceremony?

2. Explain how the increase in the divorce rate and the subsequent increase in remarriages since 1970 has affected the figures in the table.

3. The proportion of first marriages (i.e. first time for both partners) being solemnised in Register Offices has risen to one-third over the past few decades. Give reasons why this has happened.

4. 'Religious beliefs and practices are of little significance in Twentieth Century Britain.' Discuss.

11 MASS MEDIA

The Daily Telegraph

The hellish sounds of riot: alarms, sirens, breaking glass, the cries of 'Pig!'

LOOTING GANGS ROAM BRIXTON

Teenage mobs pour out to bombard police

DAILY EXPRESS
THE VOICE OF BRITAIN

Whitelaw faces the violence, then praises police bravery

RIOTS FLARE AGAIN

DAILY Mirror
THE NORTH'S BIGGEST DAILY SALE

Now street fury

Battle of Brixton

THE SHAPE OF THINGS TO COME

'The next riots will be in Birmingham and Manchester'

THE GUARDIAN
Printed in Manchester and London   Monday April 13 1981

Whitelaw promises Commons statement • Police accused of provocation • McNee reassures residents

Brixton rioting flares again as police move in

THE Sun

SHUTTLE JINX STRIKES AGAIN
— Page 5

The picture that sums up the horror of Bloody Brixton

BATTLEFRONT

THE TIMES

Mr Whitelaw expected to announce inquiry into Brixton riots today

Tiles torn away in launch of shuttle

Running battles in streets for second night

Daily Mail

More police hurt in third night of riots

NEW BATTLES HIT BRIXTON

DAILY STAR

The toll: 165 police hurt, 121 arrests

FLAMES OF HATE

FINANCIAL TIMES

Monday April 13 1981

Lovell
for Management Fee

Brixton troubles flare up again after Whitelaw visit

Bankers meet at Downing Street

U.S. back in space race

Surge of optimism among

These were the headlines in Britain's newspapers on 13 April 1981, the Monday after a weekend of rioting in Brixton, London (see Exercise 9E, pp. 74–5). Although there had been a confrontation between youths and police in Bristol a year earlier, the Brixton rioting was among the worst ever seen in mainland Britain. A few months later, serious eruptions took place in Southall (London), Toxteth (Liverpool), Moss Side (Manchester) and other urban areas (although the apparent causes and participants varied).

1. Arrange the newspapers in order of sensationalism of their headlines. Start with the newspaper with the most sensational and/or biggest (highest or boldest letters) headline and end with the newspaper with the lowest key and/or smallest headline on Brixton.

2. In what ways does this ordering reflect the general character and readership of the newspapers concerned?

3. Both the main and the smaller headlines of *The Daily Telegraph* and *The Guardian* make reference to the actions of the police and the rioters. Compare the two presentations.

4. The Home Secretary, Mr Whitelaw, visited Brixton after the rioting on the Saturday night. What does the headline in *The Financial Times* imply about the effectiveness of his visit?

5. One of Mr Whitelaw's responsibilities, as Home Secretary, is for the policing of the country. Why is his name a particularly unfortunate one in the context of areas like Brixton, Southall, Toxteth and Moss Side?

6. How is *The Daily Mirror*'s treatment of the Brixton story different from that of the other papers?

7. *The Daily Mirror*'s prophecy came true in July of the same year. In that month, Mr Whitelaw complained that people who had prophesied further troubles in Britain's inner cities after Bristol and Brixton had occurred had by their prophesying contributed to the likelihood of further riots actually taking place.
   Do you think that newspaper and television coverage can *affect* behaviour (riots, football hooliganism, demonstrations, drug use, racial conflict, legal decisions, etc.) or merely *reflect* behaviour?

Reading of national newspapers: by social class[1], 1979

	Great Britain						Percentages
	Social class of readers						Total (percentages)
	A	B	C₁	C₂	D	E	

	A	B	C_1	C_2	D	E	Total (percentages)
Daily newspapers							
Sun	1	5	18	41	29	6	100
Daily Mirror	1	6	18	41	28	7	100
Daily Express	3	15	28	31	17	6	100
Daily Mail	5	19	30	28	14	5	100
The Daily Telegraph	14	37	30	11	5	2	100
The Guardian	13	42	29	10	5	1	100
Financial Times	16	37	30	12	5	–	100
Any daily newspaper	3	13	22	33	22	7	100
Sunday newspapers:							
News of the World	1	5	17	40	29	8	100
Sunday Mirror	1	7	20	40	26	5	100
Sunday People	1	6	19	39	27	8	100
Sunday Express	6	23	30	25	12	5	100
The Observer	12	36	29	15	6	2	100
Sunday Telegraph	12	33	31	15	6	2	100
Any Sunday newspaper	3	13	22	33	22	7	100
Estimated percentage of population aged 15 plus[2]	3	13	22	32	21	9	100

[1] See Appendix, Major Surveys: National Readership Survey.
[2] Total unweighted sample 30,291.
Source: National Readership Survey 1979. *Joint Industry Committee for National Readership Surveys*

Social class in the National Readership Survey

Class A.   Upper middle class. The head of household's occupation (or former occupation) is higher managerial, administrative, or professional.

Class B.   Middle class. The head of household's occupation (or former occupation) is intermediate managerial, administrative, or professional.

Class C1.   Lower middle class. The head of household's occupation (or former occupation) is supervisory or clerical, or is junior managerial, administrative, or professional.

Class C2.   Skilled working class. Skilled manual workers.

Class D.   Working class. Semi- and unskilled manual workers.

Class E.   Those at lowest levels of subsistence. State pensioners or widows (no other earner in household), casual, or lowest grade workers.

1.   Are the members of any particular social class significantly more likely than members of other social classes to be readers of a daily or Sunday newspaper?

2.   Which daily newspaper has the highest percentage of semi-skilled and unskilled manual workers in its readership?

3. The daily and Sunday newspapers in this table are not in alphabetical order. What explanation can you give for the order in which the papers are presented?

4. Discuss the role of newspapers as moulders of public opinion.

IIC   SEXISM AND THE MEDIA

'How do you mean "saved"?'

Not a joke

☐ WELL DONE the Mirror, for drawing attention to the increasing violence against women and to the ways in which society confirms some men's views of women as sexual objects.

So I was disturbed to see a cartoon in the very same issue which trivialises rape by joking about it.—*M. Gifford, Hastings, E. Sussex.*

(From *Daily Mirror* 23 June 1981)

1. What are some of '... the ways in which society confirms some men's views of women as sexual objects'?

2. The cartoon above is 'sexist'. 'Sexism' refers not only to viewing women as sexual objects but also to all those attitudes and actions which reduce women to a minor and inferior status in society.

Write about 400 words on sexism in one or more of the following media:
(a) films,
(b) television,
(c) popular fiction (romantic novels, westerns, crime and mystery, war stories, science fiction, etc.),
(d) magazines,
(e) comics,
(f) radio.

In this poster, white segregationists showed their alarm at the increasing popularity of black music from the 1950s onwards.

NOTICE!
STOP
Help Save The Youth of America
DON'T BUY NEGRO RECORDS

(If you don't want to serve negroes in your place of business, then do not have negro records on your juke box or listen to negro records on the radio.)

The screaming, idiotic words, and savage music of these records are undermining the morals of our white youth in America.

Call the advertisers of the radio stations that play this type of music and complain to them!

Don't Let Your Children Buy, or Listen To These Negro Records

(From *The Story of the Blues* by Paul Oliver, 1972)

1. Why should southern whites feel threatened by the increasing popularity of negro music? (150 words)

2. *Research*

   Writers have pointed to the similarities between black music culture and white teenage music culture. Rock music had its beginnings in black blues/rhythm and blues. Both music forms are frequently characterised as being carefree, pleasure-seeking, authority-hating and anti-Establishment. Complaints similar to those in the poster about the 'screaming, idiotic words, and savage music of these records . . . undermining the morals of . . . youth' have been directed at many forms of teenage music over the past few decades.

   Write an essay on one of the following, discussing the extent to which that particular music/youth culture was opposed to the 'main culture' of British or American society:

   (a) rock 'n' roll in the 1950s,
   (b) flower power/psychedelic/hippie music in the late 1960s,
   (c) punks in the 1970s,
   (d) 'oi' music and skinheads,
   (e) reggae music,
   (f) another of your own choosing.